The Self-Sufficient Weaver

The Self-Sufficient Weaver

Jennifer Green

B. T. BATSFORD LTD, LONDON

ISBN 0 7134 0763 8

Typeset by D.P. Press Ltd
and printed in Great Britain by

R.J. Acford Ltd, Chichester, Sussex

for the publishers
B. T. Batsford Ltd
4 Fitzhardinge Street
London W1H 0AH

Contents

Introduction

Many people imagine that handweaving necessarily entails using massive looms, having a converted barn large enough to house all the equipment, and of course needing a large capital outlay to afford all of the above. The aim of this book is to show you that there are many ways of creating your own woven fabrics and articles using minimal equipment, most of which could be made by a skilled handyman.

If you are just beginning to weave, I would advise that you work through at least some of the techniques described in this book, before thinking about buying a large loom. The chapters have been set out in what is, I hope, a logical sequence, so that each new method of weaving introduces a slightly more complicated skill.

By concentrating on the simpler techniques to begin with, you will gradually learn the basic principles of weaving, and find the kind of things you want to make. Indeed there are so many exciting possibilities in using simple equipment, that you may well get 'hooked' on one of these types of weaving. Bearing in mind the many different kinds of yarns and colour combinations, a weaver could spend an entire career on say, inkle weaving, and never come to an end!

One important point should be mentioned — this is a practical book. Like all practical skills, it takes much longer to explain how to do something than to actually do it. So, read the directions through carefully first, but do not be discouraged if it all sounds a bit complicated. Get out your materials, have a go, and then the ideas will fall into place.

The techniques included in this book can all be done using very little equipment. Much of this can be made at home, and where appropriate there are detailed diagrams to help you to do this. If you would prefer to buy this equipment, most of it should be readily available from the suppliers listed at the end of the book.

Weaving yarns can also be bought, though to begin with odd scraps of knitting wool can be used. In case you want to make your own yarn, there is included a brief introduction to spinning on a spindle and dyeing, but there is no need to do either of these if you are just interested in the weaving. When you do buy yarn, buy the best quality that you can afford. After all, it takes time and patience to make something by hand, and you want it to give lasting pleasure. Specialist weaving yarn suppliers should be able to help you with this.

In helping to run a specialist weaving shop, it gives me great pleasure to try to advise customers on how to start weaving, and even greater pleasure when they return to show their first finished attempts. The tremendous pride with which they display their work, and the marvellous sense of achievement they feel, is something I hope the reader of this book will share.

1 Start Spinning

Before you can weave, you need yarn. Yarn can be bought, but it is much more interesting if you can create your own. Besides learning about how the yarn is constructed, there is also a tremendous feeling of achievement in knowing that, as well as weaving an article, you have also spun the wool, thus having done the whole process in turning raw fleece into a useful article.

Handspun wool has the added advantage of uneven texture. While it is every spinner's ideal to be able to spin a smooth machine-like thread (and indeed the beginner should aim for this), nevertheless the random rough-spun look of the handspun yarn can be very attractive.

WHAT IS YARN?

It is important to understand the basic principles of making a thread, as this will help when you learn to spin your own. The following instructions concentrate on woollen spinning, as fleece from the sheep is easiest to obtain, but some of the methods described can also be applied to other fibres.

If you look at a fleece when it has been shorn from the sheep, it is made up of millions of tiny loose fibres. These can easily be pulled apart by hand. However, a length of the same fleece, when spun into yarn, is much stronger. The only way the fibres cling together is by the twist inserted during the spinning process.

If you could look at one tiny fibre of fleece under a microscope, you would see that it is not smooth, but has rough nodules sticking out from it

in all directions. It is these nodules that get entwined during the twisting of the fibres, and so prevent it from un-ravelling. By the way, yarn is usually spun with the greasy fleece, so that these nodules slip over each other more easily during spinning. If the fleece has been washed, then it must be re-oiled with vegetable oil before it can be spun.

It is possible to spin yarn straight from the fleece using the fingers. Pull a small bunch of fibres from the fleece and twist them in a clockwise direction in between your fingers. As you twist, gently pull the fibres along their length until the yarn is as thin as you want it. When you have spun these fibres, gently introduce a few more at one end to make a longer piece of yarn. This is a very time-consuming process, but it is possible to spin a yarn in this way.

Did you find that the yarn broke? This shows the importance of twist in the formation of the yarn. If there is not enough twist, the yarn will easily pull apart and break. Similarly, if you pulled too quickly and the yarn became too thin with not enough twist to lock the fibres into place, then it probably snapped. On the other hand if the yarn is overtwisted, you will find it difficult to pull it out at all. Once it is locked in place and more twist is applied, you will find that the yarn will kinkle up as soon as you let it go. By doing these experiments you can see that the amount of twist introduced into the fibres plays a crucial part in making a good finished yarn. It is only with practice that you will get the feel of this and be able to judge it more easily.

Of course there are serious disadvantages to using this method of spinning straight from the fleece, without any preparation. The first is that it takes a very long time to make enough yarn to be useful. However, more important than this is the fact that any pieces of dirt left in the fleece are trapped in the spun yarn, so you are bound to get a rather lumpy yarn, unless your fleece happens to be particularly clean. In order to speed up the process and produce a more even yarn, it is much better to use a spindle and to prepare the fleece as explained below.

OBTAINING FLEECE

If you have your own sheep, obtaining fleece is no problem. Alternatively you may know a local farmer who has sheep. However, in England he is required by law to send his fleece to the British Wool Marketing Board, though he is allowed to keep up to four fleece for his own use. Shearing time is usually around June or July depending on the weather, so an approach to the farmer some time before this may be worth a try. Fleece can also be obtained from the British Wool Marketing Board direct or from specialist suppliers (addresses at the end of the book).

Picking pieces of fleece off the fences and hedges in the spring is great fun (though the farmer's permission should be obtained first) and is a really good way to interest children in undertaking a spinning project. However, it is not easy to start spinning using this fleece, as it contains only short fibres and matted locks, torn from the sheep as it rubs against the fences. It seems like sacrilege to say this, but when you begin, get a really good fleece. Spinning is not easy until you have had some practice, and it makes it even more difficult if you have to contend with difficult fleece as well. One can liken spinning to swimming or riding a bicycle — it seems very difficult at first, but is easy once you know how!

Fleece from the hedgerows can be a good source of free raw material, but apart from the difficulties mentioned above, it takes time to collect enough to make a useful article. If you are seriously interested in learning to spin, it is better to invest in a good fleece, or better still, think about keeping some sheep of your own.

The type of fleece you choose for spinning is important. There are over thirty different sheep breeds in the British Isles, and these can roughly be divided into three groups:

a long staple, with a fibre length of 15 cm (6 in) or more.
b medium staple, with a fibre length of about 10–15 cm (4–6 in).
c short staple, with a fibre length of under 10 cm (4 in).

The sheep with the longest coats are the hill or mountain sheep, as the animals need good protection against the harsh winter climate. These fleece also tend to have a coarse texture, such as the Herdwick and Swaledale breeds (from the Lake District and Yorkshire respectively), and the wool is used for carpets or made into strong hardwearing outer garments. The sheep from the downland areas are much softer, and their fleece length is much shorter. One example of this is the Southdown fleece. The Merino sheep from Australia are also soft and have a short staple length, so their fleece is ideal for fine soft knitwear.

A medium length staple is usually best for the beginner. Those fleece with a fibre length of 10–15 cm (4–6 in) are the easiest to handle. Good fleece for a beginner are Clun Forest, Portland and Jacob. The Jacob is very popular with handspinners as it is a white sheep with brown patches on it. The proportions of the different colours vary with each sheep, but the spinner has the choice of separating the brown from the white and spinning two different coloured yarns from one fleece, or blending them together to obtain a third colour, grey. A variety of natural colours can therefore be obtained and combined in the weaving to form interesting patterns, without the need for any dyeing.

MAKING A SPINDLE

A spindle at its most basic is simply a stick and a weight, usually joined together in some way. It enables the fibres to be spun much faster than by hand, leaving the spinner's hands free to manipulate the yarn.

A bamboo cane is used in the example, simply because it is easier for an inexperienced woodworker to cut the slit in the top from this, as it has a natural hole down the centre. It also tapers at one end, and can be cut so that the whorl (round weight at the bottom) can rest on one of the nodes of the cane. If a dowel is used, this should be tapered towards the top so that the whorl does not drop off the bottom, and a hole drilled into the top before beginning to cut the slit as shown in the diagram.

Choose a bamboo that is straight and has as long a distance as possible between each node. Cut the cane just under two of the nodes, so that one node forms the base on which the

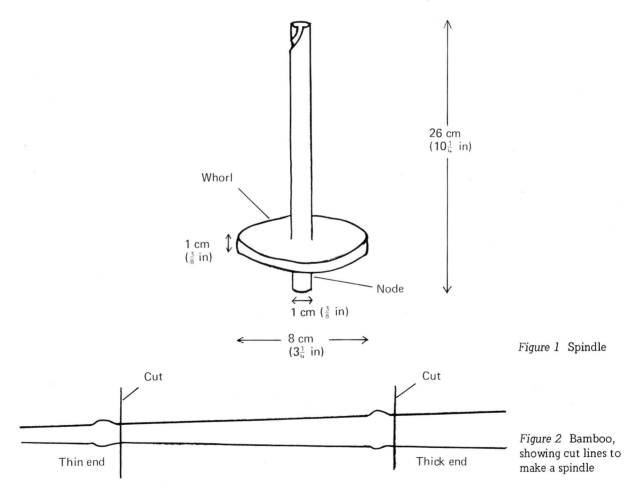

26 cm
($10\frac{1}{4}$ in)

Whorl

1 cm
($\frac{3}{8}$ in)

Node

1 cm ($\frac{3}{8}$ in)

8 cm
($3\frac{1}{4}$ in)

Figure 1 Spindle

Cut

Cut

Thin end

Thick end

Figure 2 Bamboo, showing cut lines to make a spindle

9

whorl can rest. The exact size and shape of the whorl is not crucial, but it must be well balanced, so that the spindle spins easily. A cross-piece of wood is an equally good alternative. The hole in the whorl should be drilled exactly in the centre, and the whorl should fit fairly tightly on to the shaft, resting on the bottom node. The whorl can be stuck down if there is likely to be any movement in it while spinning.

The cutting of the slit at the top is important as the spun yarn must pass easily through this, so there should be no rough edges on which it could catch. The disadvantage with bamboo is that it can break rather easily at this point, so that if you want to do a lot of spinning, it might be as well to make or buy a wooden one. Bamboo, however, is ideal to begin with. One word of warning if you do buy one — many spindles just have a notch at the top which means that the yarn has to be secured with a slip knot every time you wind on, thus taking up unnecessary time. If you cannot get one with a slit, it is better to make your own or have one made for you. The spindle with a slit also spins better as the yarn

comes up from the exact centre of the shaft.

PREPARING THE FLEECE FOR SPINNING

As mentioned above, fleece is usually spun in its natural greasy state. This helps the fibres to slip over each other more easily as the fleece is pulled out prior to spinning. Some people find that they do not like the feel of the dirty greasy fleece, or the smell! In fact the natural lanolin in the fleece is very good for the hands. If you decide that you must wash the fleece before spinning (if it is particularly dirty or if you want to dye it before spinning), this must be done very, very carefully. Use soapflakes (detergent will whiten the fleece) in hand-hot water, handling the fleece as little as possible, and leaving it spread out in the garden to dry naturally. An alternative method is to soak the fleece in cold water; this removes the dirt, but leaves the natural oil in the fleece. Whichever method you use, if you are not very careful, the fibres will become felted (matted together) and will be very difficult to pull apart for spinning. One important point to note is that if the oil has been removed by washing, the fleece must be re-oiled with vegetable oil (olive oil is best) before it can be spun.

The first preparation necessary before the wool can be spun is called teasing. This process involves pulling apart the fibres so that any bits of dirt lodged in the fleece drop out and do not get caught up in the finished yarn. Pull a small bunch of fibres from the fleece and hold them in your left hand, with one end of the fibres held by the fingers and thumb and the other end between the fingers and the palm of the hand. Keep the fibres fairly taut. With the right hand pull away a few fibres at a time, letting any dirt drop on to the floor. Incidentally, this process can be fairly messy, so it is best to wear an apron to protect your

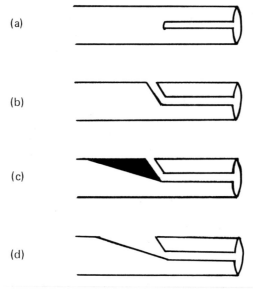

(a)

(b)

(c)

(d)

Figure 3 Cutting the slit in the top of the spindle

clothes and put newspaper on the floor. It is a good occupation to do in the garden on a sunny day, but not if it is windy, as the light fleece may blow away!

Put the teased fleece into a pile to one side of where you are teasing. I have seen spinners carefully letting the dirt from the fleece being teased drop back into what they have already teased! The object of the exercise is to get rid of the little bits of dirt and grit that the sheep inevitably picks up. Even on what looks like a fairly clean fleece, it is surprising what a great deal of dirt is eliminated at this stage.

The difference between the raw and teased fleece should be apparent when you have finished. What before were tightly packed locks of fleece are now an airy pile of soft curls. The air is an important part of the finished woollen yarn, so do not squash this pile. Use a large cardboard box or a sack (not plastic) so that the air is retained at this stage.

The next step is to get all the fibres parallel to one another ready for spinning. Ideally this should be done with carders, but as these are rather expensive to buy or make, the method outlined below does not necessitate their use. It is not an ideal method and if you can get hold of a pair of carders and learn to use them, this is better. To begin with, however, try the method without them.

Take hold of the wool fibres and carefully arrange some of them in a parallel line on your lap. The fibres should be arranged closely together, in a row of about 15–20 cm (6–8 in) long. The more care you take at this stage to arrange the fibres, the easier the spinning will be. When you have this rolag in a reasonably tidy state, gently roll it up. Start at the edge on the right and lightly roll, so that the fibres run around and around the rolag when it is completed. You should end up with a sausage-shaped object with

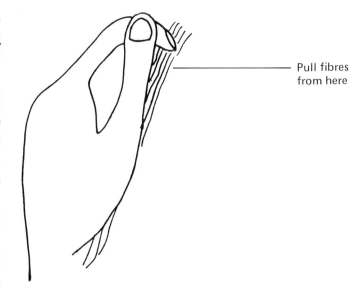

Figure 4 Holding the fleece while teasing

Pull fibres from here

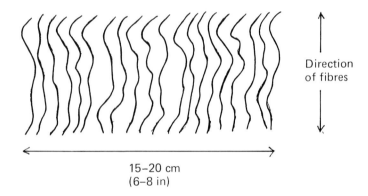

Direction of fibres

15–20 cm (6–8 in)

Figure 5 Rolag

a diameter of about 2–5 cm (1–2 in). If the rolag is too thick, it will be difficult to spin, as it will not pull apart easily, and if it is too thin it will break. Adjust the amount of fleece you use in your rolags and you will soon find the size that you find easiest to spin.

As with the teased fibres, it is very important that these rolags keep their light and airy texture, as it is the air spun into the yarn that gives wool its fluffy texture and makes clothes made from wool such good body warmers.

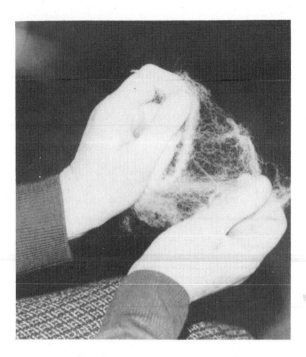

Photograph 1 Teasing the fleece

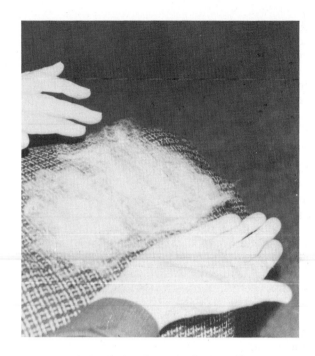

Photograph 2 Placing fleece ready for rolling

Photograph 3 Making a rolag

Photograph 4 Finished rolag

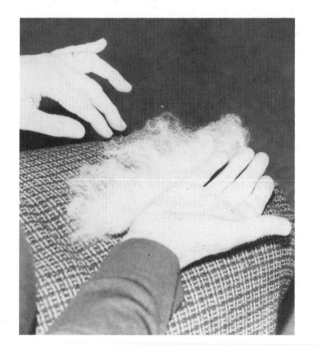

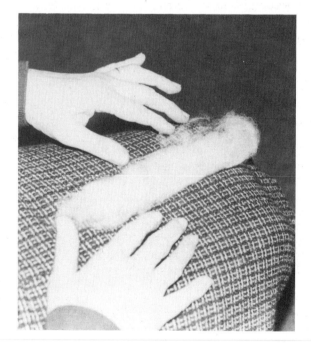

A large cardboard box is the best place to keep the rolags, so that they do not get squashed.

Before you actually begin to spin, make sure that you have a large pile of rolags ready made, as the actual spinning is fairly quick, and you will probably not want to keep stopping to make more rolags.

SPINNING ON A SPINDLE

Having made a spindle as described above, the first stage is to wrap a starter thread around the shaft. Make a length of handspun wool, twisting it in your fingers as described above, or use an oddment of knitting wool. Using a piece at least a metre (yard) long, wrap it around the shaft of the spindle in an anti-clockwise direction. Begin at the base of the shaft just above the whorl, and when this thread is firmly anchored, wind the rest of it quickly up the shaft and slip it into the notch at the top. Leave at least 30 cm (12 in) of thread sticking out of the notch at the top.

Take this spare length of spun yarn in your left hand, letting the spindle hang down from it. With your right hand, grip the shaft of the spindle and twist it in a clockwise direction. Check that the spindle is evenly balanced and continues to spin for a little while before reversing.

In order to help join the spun fibres to the unspun, take the end of the starter thread and just untwist the end fibres, fanning them out a little at the end. You will see how this machine-spun yarn is made up of loose fibres just like the fleece. To get a smooth join it is important that the spun and the unspun fibres are only slowly introduced to each other. If you do any knitting, splicing a join in the middle of a row is quite a good comparison.

Take the first rolag in your left hand and, holding near one end with the thumb and fingers, let the bulk of the rolag hang over the back of the

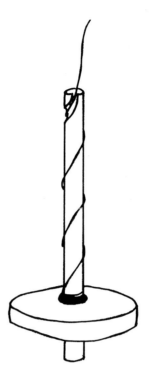

Figure 6 Starting thread wound on spindle

hand. In doing this it is kept well away from the spinning spindle and should not get caught up accidentally. Hold the starter thread also in your left hand so that the spindle hangs down freely. You need to keep the right hand free at this stage to spin the spindle, but once it is spinning, the right hand holds the starter thread and assists in controlling the amount of spin that reaches the unspun rolag.

When the spindle is turning, hold the starter thread tightly in the right hand, about 22 cm (9 in) from the top of the spindle. Pull the beginning of the rolag gently apart and introduce some of the fibres from it into the starter thread. Relax your grip slightly and let a small amount of spin pass through the right hand, just enough to anchor the fibres.

After the rolag is joined, the act of drawing out the rolag and letting the spin into the fibres to make a yarn.

should, with practice, become an easy rhythmical action — remember the comparison with riding a bicycle! Hold the rolag in the left hand and the yarn tightly in the right about 22 cm (9 in) above the top of the spindle, making sure that the spindle is still spinning clockwise. Rehold about 8 cm (3 in) further up the rolag and gently pull the fibres until the yarn is fairly even and about the thickness you require. Then let the spin which has built up on the spun yarn travel up the unspun thread by gently releasing your right hand grip. Next rehold the yarn about 8 cm (3 in) further up, pull out a few more fibres and continue the above sequence.

While all this is going on, remember to keep checking that the spindle is still revolving, and in the right direction! Once you have established a rhythm and are fairly proficient, this will become part of the cycle, but to begin with, keep looking, or even get a friend to help you by keeping the spindle turning. There is nothing more annoying than having drawn a perfect length of fibres, only to find it breaks because there is no spin left to hold the fibres in place.

If all this sounds a little like keeping all the plates balanced on poles in a circus act, then I am afraid that it probably is at the beginning. Spinning is not easy. It is a skill that has to be learned and, like all skills, it does look effortless when demonstrated by an expert. The only advice I can give is to keep practising, and not give up just because you find it difficult at first.

Having spun a metre (yard) of yarn, you will find that you have to hold the spindle up high in order to prevent it touching the floor. At this point, lift up the spindle in your right hand

Photograph 5 Spinning on a spindle

and unwind the yarn round the top of the shaft. If the yarn kinkles back on itself as soon as the tension is released, wind it up in a figure of eight on to your left thumb and index finger before unhitching the yarn from the spindle. Wind the spun yarn on top of the starter thread at the base of the spindle shaft, leaving enough thread to wind up the shaft and still have about 30 cm (12 in) to spare at the top. Then continue spinning again. This process of spinning and winding can be repeated until there is a good wedge of yarn on the spindle. When it becomes too heavy the yarn may break more easily as it is drawn out.

Remove the spun yarn from the spindle when it is full, skein it and then wash it to remove the oil. (Directions for this are given in the next chapter under 'Preparing the yarn'.) If you want to keep the natural oils in the wool, then use a cold water wash to remove the dirt but not the oil.

PLYING

Whether or not to ply the handspun yarn depends on the use to which it will be put. If it is to be knitted, then it is better plied, as a singles yarn sometimes tends to end up with the garment distorted sideways. A plied yarn is thicker and tends to give a more even yarn, as the thicker lumps and the thin parts may even out against one another.

To ply handspun wool, wind the yarn off the spindle into two balls. Note that it is better to ply the yarn before it is washed, but the method described below can also be applied to clean yarn and machinespun yarn.

The construction of the yarn is important. When spinning on a spindle, with the spindle rotated in a clockwise direction, the yarn produced is known as 'Z' spun yarn, because of the direction in which the fibres run. The spindle should be turned in the opposite direction to ply the wool. If you find this

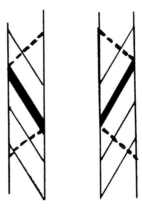

Figure 7 'S' and 'Z' spin

difficult on the spindle with the slit at the top, it might be worthwhile making another spindle with the slit cut in the opposite direction; this spindle can then be kept especially for plying.

The two balls of singles wool should be put into two separate boxes or waste-paper baskets, in order to prevent them getting tangled. These should be placed to the left of the standing spinner. Tie the two ends on to the starter thread on the spindle, remembering to rewind this thread on the spindle in the opposite direction before you start plying. Hold the two threads of yarn over your left hand, keeping them apart with a finger. Spin the spindle in an anti-clockwise direction and let the two threads pass through the fingers fairly quickly.

You will notice that the threads do not need much twist to make them ply together, so you should be careful not to overtwist them, and keep stopping to wind the plied yarn on to the spindle shaft. As you will see, plying is much quicker than spinning. When the spindle gets too heavy, wind off the yarn and wash it.

Interesting yarns can also be created by plying. If you have spun Jacob wool, try plying one strand of the natural white with one strand of the brown. Of course you can ply as many threads together as you want, in order to make a thicker yarn, the only limitation being the difficulty of a thick yarn to slip into the notch at the top of the spindle.

SPINNING FOR WEAVING
The uneven texture of the handspun yarns means that, at least at the beginning, it will be difficult to use them in the warp (the threads set up first on the loom). However, the textured handspun yarn is ideal for weft (the threads woven at right angles to the warp), as the uneven quality can produce interesting surface textures.

A plied handspun yarn can be used for warp, as this is more even than a singles yarn, though in some cases it may be too thick for the purpose desired. In the following chapters suitable types of yarn for various projects have been indicated, and where your handspun fits these criteria, it is a good idea to use it.

However, when you start weaving, it is probably better to experiment with odd scraps of knitting wool, rather than risk using your precious handspun if you are not sure of the result.

2 Dyeing Handspun Wool

The natural colours of the fleece are beautiful by themselves and range from natural white to dark brown (natural black), with many different shades of browns and greys in between. However, in order to introduce a little more colour into your work, handspun yarns can be dyed using vegetable or chemical dyes. For this it is best to start with the natural white wool, though interesting effects may be obtained by overdyeing light coloured fleece (grey or light brown).

To some extent natural dyeing is a rather hit-and-miss process, as it is never possible to repeat an exact colour. Part of the excitement of dyeing is that you never quite know what shade you will end up with! Natural dyeing is a vast subject in its own right, and though this chapter forms a very limited introduction only, nevertheless it should encourage you to experiment further.

PREPARING THE YARN
It is vital that the handspun wool is thoroughly washed before dyeing. Any oil left in the wool will prevent the dye from being fully absorbed into the fibres, and thus the yarn may turn out rather patchy in colour. Machinespun yarn can of course also be dyed, but it should be washed first if there is any likelihood of its being greasy.

The yarn must be skeined. If it were left in a ball, the outer yarn would be dyed, while the inside would stay white as the dye would be unable to penetrate the outer layers of the ball.

You want the dye to be applied evenly, therefore the yarn must be free to move in the dyebath, but without getting tangled.

Make a skein by winding the wool over your hand and bent elbow, or round the back of a chair. Tie the ends loosely around the skein. To make sure that the skein does not break free during washing or dyeing, insert two more ties, this time in a figure of eight. Any yarn can be used to make these ties (cotton, linen or wool) but *not* a coloured yarn, as the colour might run. It is important that these ties are inserted very loosely, so that they do not prevent the dye reaching parts of the yarn. If you deliberately tie them too tightly it will produce a tie-and-dye effect.

Wash the wool carefully by hand using soapflakes — detergent will tend to whiten the wool. Hang the skein up

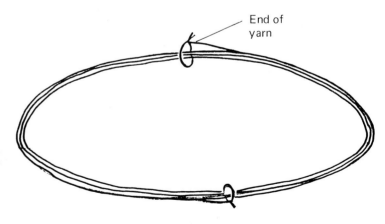

End of yarn

Figure 8 Skein, showing ends tied back on each other

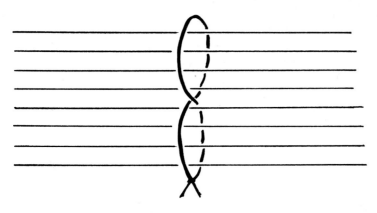

Figure 9 Figure of eight tie

Photograph 6 The dyepot

to dry naturally, and suspend a weight from the bottom of the skein to stop the yarn kinkling. A medium-sized stone tied to the skein with string is ideal. Incidentally, if you intend to dye the wool straight after washing, there is no need to dry it first.

EQUIPMENT NEEDED FOR DYEING

Dyeing takes a long time, with the water having to be kept hot for up to several hours. A small electric or oil stove which can safely be left un-attended for some time is best. I would recommend that you do your dyeing in the garden in fine weather or in an outhouse, rather than in the kitchen, not only because the smell can be rather unpleasant, but also so that the chemicals used can be kept well away from food.

You will need a large receptacle in which to boil the dyestuff. Stainless steel is the best for this, as the metal will not affect the dye colour. An enamel bowl or an old fish kettle are also quite good, as is any heat-resistant container you have around, the larger the better so you can dye enough wool at one time to make it worthwhile.

Other essential items are a long stick or wooden spoon to stir the dye-bath occasionally, and a pair of rubber gloves so that you don't end up with dyed fingers as well!

To get the best colour from the dyestuff, soft water or rain water is best. Rain water is most easily collect-ed from a water butt.

Weighing scales are also important for measuring dyestuffs and mordants. They need to have fairly close divisions to weigh the small quantities of mor-dants, but a large bowl is helpful to weigh the actual dyestuff as, generally speaking, it needs the same weight of dyestuff to the amount of wool you want to dye. Imagine what a huge pile of onion skins you need in order to dye half a kilo (one pound) of wool! Now you can see why the bigger the dyebath the better, so you can dye enough yarn at one time.

USING DYESTUFFS FOUND IN THE HOME

Most dyestuffs require a mordant. This is simply a chemical that will make the wool accept the dye more readily, and the methods for using it are described in the next section.

There are a number of items which can easily be obtained and which dye very well without a mordant. These are known as substantive dyes. Turmeric produces a very bright yellow, though unfortunately it is not a very permanent colour. Wood chips will also dye without a mordant, as will lichen. Both of these produce pale brown colours.

The general method for dyeing yarn is as follows:

a Put the yarn and the dyestuff into the dyebath and add just enough water to cover them.

b Put the bath on the heat and slowly bring the water up to simmer. It should not be allowed to boil.

c Simmer for anything from about half an hour to about two hours, until the wool looks as though it has accepted enough dye. You may need to add more water during this time if it evaporates too much. The skein of yarn should be carefully turned from time to time in order to help distribute the dye evenly.

d Remove the skein from the water and rinse in warm water until all the excess dye has been removed, and hang it up to dry.

Remember that, as when washing woollen knitwear, care must be taken at all times. Try not to handle the wool too much and *never* plunge the cold wool into hot water.

Incidentally, here is one tip if you are using dyes such as lichen or wood chips, where little bits of these are likely to get mixed with the wool — put the dyestuff in a muslin bag and then put this into the dyebath. It saves time afterwards as you will not have to pick all the little pieces of dyestuff out of the dyed skein!

MORDANTS

By using mordants, the range of natural materials which can be successfully dyed increases tremendously. Virtually any plant can be used to produce some sort of dye, though mainly they produce dull yellows and browns. Mordanting the wool also helps to make the colour more permanent and, by using different mordants with the same dyestuffs, it is possible to obtain different shades from the one dyebath.

Alum (potassium aluminium sulphate) is the most readily obtainable mordant, and may be available from a local chemist. It is important to weigh the mordant carefully before use, as only a very small amount is needed. For alum, use about 85 g (3 oz) alum for every 450 g (1 lb) of wool you want to dye. You can put the mordant in with the dyestuff and thus mordant and dye at the same time. However, while it does save time, the results are not so good as mordanting separately before dyeing begins.

To mordant with alum, first dissolve the alum in a little boiling water. Then add this to the clean water in the dyebath. Wet the wool, and put it in the dyebath when the water temperature is warm. Simmer the wool for about an hour, giving the bath an occasional stir with a stick or wooden spoon. Gently remove the wool from the dyebath and let it drain, if necessary squeezing gently to remove any surplus water.

The wool can be dyed immediately or kept until you are ready to dye it. You can mordant several skeins of wool at the same time, and then dye them with different dyestuffs later on. However, if you decide to keep several mordanted skeins, then do label them carefully, so you know for your records which mordant was used on which skein.

The other common mordants are chrome (potassium dichromate), iron (ferrous sulphate) and tin (stannous chloride), but you will probably have to obtain these from a specialist supplier. These mordants are more difficult to use than alum. Chrome, for example, is very sensitive to light, so that the wool must be kept covered while being dyed. Care should be taken with these mordants and the amount used should be weighed as accurately as possible, using only approximately 7 g (¼ oz) to every 450 g (1 lb) of wool. The advantage of using several different mordants is that you can, for example, put one skein of wool mordanted in each of the different mordants into one dyebath, and thus obtain four different shades from the one lot of dyestuff. Colours ranging from dark orange to brown can be obtained if you use onion skins in this way.

OTHER DYESTUFFS
Generally speaking it is worth trying to dye with most plants and vegetables. The greatest limitation for the home dyer is the amount of each dyestuff that is available, bearing in mind that you need about 450 g (1 lb) of dyestuff for the same amount of wool.

Many of the household waste products that are usually thrown away can be utilized as dyestuffs. Coffee grounds and tea leaves both produce brownish colours. Carrot peelings give a pale green, and lemon peel will produce yellow. However, some vegetables produce rather surprising results, such as tomato mordanted with alum, which makes a pale lemon shade!

You can also try dyeing with flowers, either using the flower head by itself, or the leaves, or even both together. Golden rod is a particularly good dye source, producing colours from pale to bright yellow/green depending on the mordant used.

Most of these natural dyestuffs should be used with a mordant. Many of them will produce shades of light brown and pale yellow, and a little experimenting will soon show which plants are more successful than others.

CHEMICAL DYES
The natural dyes produce some very interesting and subtle shades, but if you prefer brighter colours with less of a hit-and-miss reaction, then you might consider chemical dyeing.

On a small scale it is not worth investing in all the different chemicals needed, and there are some excellent domestic dyes on the market, usually available in small quantities from hardware shops. There is usually a wide range of colours to choose from, and if you want your wool dyed a particular shade, then this is a more certain way to achieve a successful result.

If you want to carry on and experiment further along these lines, then there are some good chemical dye kits on the market, enabling the home dyer to mix small amounts of dye accurately and thus create the desired shade more easily.

KEEPING RECORDS
The success of your dyeing with vegetable dyes depends on keeping accurate records. It is no use producing a lovely shade and then having no idea as to how to repeat it! On the other hand, failures should also be noted so that in the future, time is not wasted on something where the result was not successful.

When keeping records, it is important to note the following information:

a The name of the dyestuff and what parts of the plant were used (flowers only, leaves only, or both?).
b What mordant (if any) was used and the quantity.

c What yarn was used — if handspun, note down the type of fleece.
d How much water was used and where it was obtained (rainwater, soft tap water?).
e Outline the method of mordanting and the dyeing process, including as much detail as possible, noting the time taken at each step (for how long was the dyepot boiled, etc?).

You can see that a dye recipe is similar to a cookery recipe, first listing all the ingredients and then the instructions for use, so that someone else (or yourself at a later date) could duplicate the experiment and hope to achieve a similar result.

Lastly, and most importantly, a sample of dyed wool should be attached to the sheet of paper. It is all very well trying to describe colour, but there is no substitute for the real thing!

3 What is Weaving?

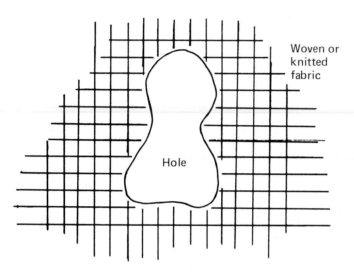

Figure 10 Hole in fabric

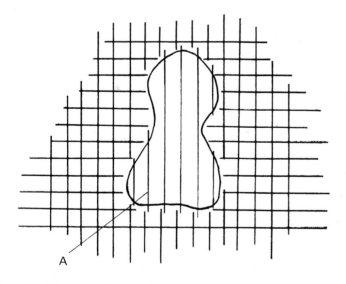

Figure 11 Warp threads across hole

Having spun and dyed your own wool, you are now all ready to get weaving. Most people can recognize if a piece of fabric has been woven, but it is more difficult to define exactly what weaving is. The most common definition is that weaving is the interlacement of two sets of threads at an angle of about ninety degrees. This definition is fine for a dictionary, but it is not very helpful to the person who wants to know more about weaving. In explaining to people what weaving really is, I prefer to use the comparison with darning.

In order to fill in a hole in a ready-made garment (see figures 10–12), first of all a set of parallel threads is sewn across the hole (A). In weaving, this is equivalent to the *warp* threads which are set up on the loom and form the foundation of the weaving.

When a row of these threads has been completed all the way across the hole, another thread (B) is darned in with a needle, at right angles to the first set of threads. The needle is taken over the first 'A' thread and under the second, and this sequence is repeated until the end of the row.

The thread for the second 'B' row takes the alternate course to the first 'B' row. So, a thread that passed over an 'A' thread in the first row now goes under it in the second row. This sequence is repeated so that all the threads in the second 'B' row are offset, rather like bricks in a wall.

Each row of 'B' threads is pushed down close to the previous row, thus forming a solid piece of fabric in what was the hole.

22

If we can take this comparison with weaving even further, we can see that the original piece of fabric with the hole in it forms the 'loom' — a 'loom' can loosely be defined as anything that will hold a parallel set of threads in place, prior to weaving. This first set of threads is known as the 'warp', with the set of threads woven across (the 'weft') forming a solid piece of material. What is achieved by darning is that another piece of material has been woven across the hole.

If you can keep this idea in mind while reading the rest of this book, it may help you to understand that all the different types of weaving are really only variations on this theme. The different looms used vary from a simple frame, a piece of cardboard or a table loom, to the more complicated jacquard looms used in commercial cloth production.

The yarn which passes over the warp threads to make the piece of material is simply threaded over and under these threads. Because of the different ways of doing this (for example, over one/under one, over two/under two, etc.) it is possible to create different patterns in the weave. The function of 'heddles' and 'shafts' is to save the weaver the laborious task of threading each individual row by hand.

What I have described as darning is

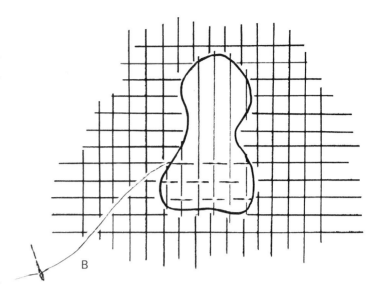

Figure 12 Darning in weft threads to form new fabric

really only a basic form of needle-weaving. The disadvantage of darning is that it is designed to be left on the loom (the piece of material that surrounds the hole). If we want to create a piece of fabric that can be woven and then removed from the loom, clearly we have to explore other ways of holding the warp threads in position. The chapters that follow show how this can be done.

4 Finger Weaving

The first kind of weaving that is presented here requires no specialized equipment and is easily portable. Using thick yarn you can quickly make braids and bands, which can be used for belts, ties, etc., or sewn together to make larger articles.

EQUIPMENT NEEDED

You can probably find all the items you need around the house.

a A small stick or pencil around which to anchor the yarn before weaving.

b Something on which to tie the warp ends while weaving and which is firm enough not to move when you pull on the yarn to bring it under tension — a door knob or the back of a heavy chair are ideal.

c A tape measure to measure the lengths of yarn.

d Scissors to cut the yarn.

e Yarn — to start with use a thick handknitting wool. If you have any odd scraps left over from knitting garments, it is a good idea to use them. The wool should be at least double-double knitting thickness or thicker. Later on you can use finer wool, but to begin with it is better to make something quick and simple until you get the hang of the weaving technique. The wool must be smooth (so that it does not stick) and if you do decide to try your handspun wool later on, it should be plied first.

Having assembled the items you need, try weaving a band as described below.

WEAVING A BAND

Before you can actually start the weaving process, you have to set up the 'loom'. Do not rush this stage, as the more carefully you set it up, the easier you will find it to weave.

Cut about thirty lengths of wool, at least two and a half times the finished length you require. So for a tie belt of about 175 cm (70 in) including fringe, measure and cut the lengths about 440 cm (175 in) long. Remember it is better to be slightly overgenerous on the length, than to find you have a woven band that is not quite long enough for what you wanted! Assuming you make a belt as above, you will need about 75 g (3 oz) of double-double knitting wool.

For your first band I would suggest you cut half the lengths in one colour and the other half in a good contrasting colour. The two colours will be referred to as black and white here for convenience, but provided you have a good contrast it makes no difference what colours you use.

Having cut the right number of lengths, take the first black thread, fold it over in the middle and wrap it around the stick, as shown in figure 13. Pull it tight around the stick and make sure that the yarn is evenly divided in half. Then take a white thread and do the same, laying it close up against the first thread. Continue doing this, using alternate black and white threads, until all the threads are mounted on the stick.

You will see that half the threads

Figure 13 Warp threads wrapped around stick

come off the stick one side and half come off the other side (marked 'A' and 'B' in figure 13). Take the 'A' set of threads (it does not really matter which set of threads you take, but I will call them 'A' and 'B' for clarity) and bunching them together, tie them securely on to a door knob or chair. Make sure that when you pull on the 'B' threads, the 'A' threads do not come undone.

In finger weaving, the actual weaving process starts at what will be the middle of the finished band (where the stick is now), and having woven one half of the band (the 'B' threads), the stick is taken out and the band is completed by weaving up the 'A' threads. The stick inserted at the beginning serves two functions: first it keeps the threads in order at this stage, and second it forms a rigid bar up to which the weft threads are pushed.

To weave, take the 'B' threads in your left hand and hold them taut. With the right hand, pick up all the white (alternate) threads near the stick, keeping the ends of all the 'B' threads in your left hand. The space between the two sets of threads is where the weft thread passes and it is this thread that holds the band together. Finger weaving is rather unusual in that the thread on the far left of the weaving is passed through the warp and is then taken down to rejoin the

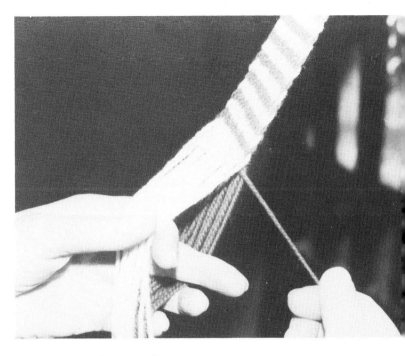

Photograph 7 Fingerweaving

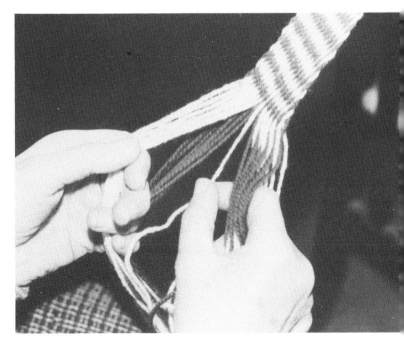

Photograph 8 Changing the shed from white threads on top to black threads on top

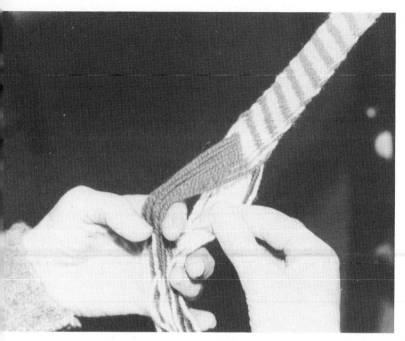

Photograph 9 Pulling the weft through the shed

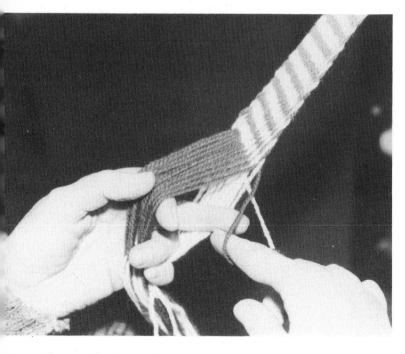

Photograph 10 Putting the previous black weft thread back into the warp

other warp threads when it reaches the right of the band. Also in this type of weaving, it is only the warp threads that will show in the finished band — this is known as a warp-faced band.

So, keeping the black and white threads apart by inserting your right hand between them, take hold of the thread on the far left of the warp in your right fingers, pull it out of your left hand and as you retract your right hand, bring this thread across the warp until it sticks out at the right hand side of the weaving. Now complete the first row of weaving, by pushing this weft thread as close up to the stick as possible, though do not worry if it will not go very near or will not stay in place — the next weft thread will secure it.

The second weft row involves the alternate set of threads. Again, keeping the 'B' threads taut in the left hand, this time pick up all the black threads in your right fingers and pull the thread which is now on the far left, through to join the first weft thread on the right. Push the second weft thread up near the first weft thread.

Now because you want the finished band to have a selvedge on both sides, twist the first thread around the second weft thread and bring it down to rejoin the other warp threads by holding it in the left hand once again.

At this point you will begin to see that in order to keep the selvedges even, and to produce a nice tightly woven band, tension plays a very important part. Before you insert the first weft thread back into the warp, pull it so that all the warp threads at that point lie close up next to each other and you cannot see the weft thread running in between. However, do not worry if your first rows are not very even, because as the band is woven from the middle, you can unpick these few rows later on, before you weave up the 'A' threads.

Repeat the weaving process as described above, lifting white threads one row and black threads the next, and for each row taking the left hand thread over to the right. Continue weaving until you come near the end of the warp threads or until the band itself is half as long as you require.

In order to stop the end from coming undone, it is just as well to finish it off at this stage. Depending on what the band is to be used for, the ends can be plaited or twisted together in groups of three of four threads, knotting the ends of these groups to keep the twists or plaits in place. Alternatively you can oversew the ends, but if you are not sure how you want to complete the band at this stage, just tie several knots at the end to stop it unravelling, making sure that they are loose enough to remove easily later on.

Having woven half the band, untie the 'A' threads from the door knob and discard the stick. Turn the band around and tie the woven half to the door knob. Making sure that the stripes are all running in the same direction, start weaving the 'A' threads, continuing the woven band from the middle. At this stage you can unpick the first row or two of weaving if you were not happy with the result.

Weave the second half of the band as described above for the 'B' threads and finish off.

COLOUR AND PATTERN VARIATIONS
The band described above with alternate threads of black and white produces diagonal stripes across the width of the band. This is due to the colour arrangement of the warp threads. Because the band is woven in plain weave (as in darning, over one thread and under the next), the only variations in pattern are possible by colour changes, and this is where this simple technique has endless possibilities.

A plain band with spots of colour is

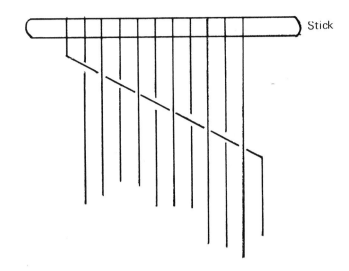

Figure 14 Path of first warp thread

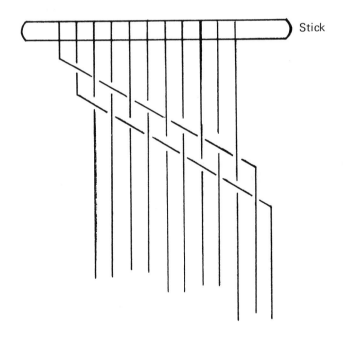

Figure 15 Path of second warp thread

possible by making the warp nearly all one colour, but introducing one row of a contrasting colour just here and there, say every fifth row. Because the warp thread goes under and over the weft

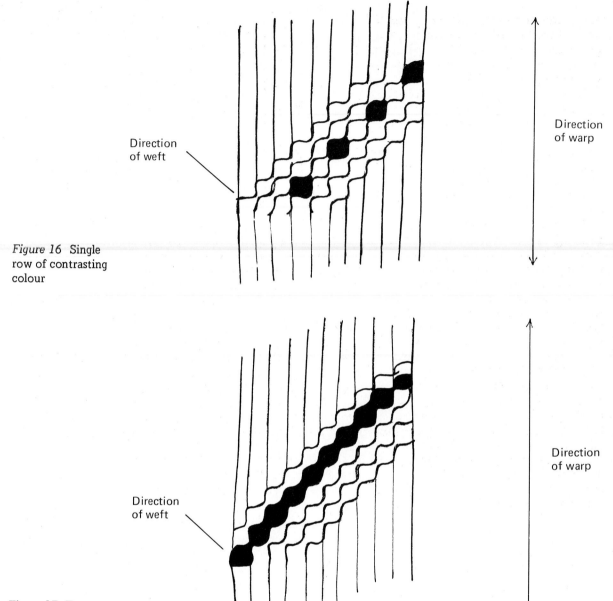

Direction of weft

Direction of warp

Figure 16 Single row of contrasting colour

Direction of weft

Direction of warp

Figure 17 Two rows of contrasting colour

thread, the contrast colour will not make a continuous line, but will appear as short dashes on the band. For more spots, add more single rows of contrast in more than one colour if you like, and for less add just one or two warp threads like this.

To make a definite stripe of colour appear to go diagonally along the length of the band, use two threads of contrast next to each other. One thread will show in one row and the other will appear in the next, thus making a continuous line. The thicker the stripe you want, the more threads you should group together of one colour. There are tremendous possibilities of using different colours and widths of stripes to create variation.

So far, weaving diagonally from left to right only has been mentioned. When you start to weave the second half of the band, if you get it upside-down, the diagonal will change direction. This can be used as a decorative effect in, for example, a belt, where half the diagonals go one way and half go the other.

There are many other ways of finger weaving, which involve weaving with more than one thread at one time, and weaving from the sides to the middle across the band. If you are interested in exploring some of these possibilities, find a detailed book on this subject to help you or just go on and experiment on your own.

IDEAS FOR WEAVING

Because these bands sometimes tend to be rather loose in construction, their use is rather limited. Belts are a good starting point. I have made quite a few of these, just plaiting the ends in small groups and letting them hang down in a decorative fringe. The advantage of these types of belt is that they will fit anyone!

Figure 18 Finger-woven bands sewn together

Men's ties can be made, though a thinner wool would be better for this, and the ends should be neatly over-sewn, or hemmed back into the band.

If you decide that you want to make larger items, the bands can be sewn together. Matching the stripes in the bands can be a problem, but if you sew them so that the diagonals deliberately oppose each other they do not need to be matched so carefully.

Tunics can be made using the bands, though more complicated garments are not really possible as the bands will easily come to pieces if they are cut. Bags are a good idea, but they are better lined, and a good strong twisted cord for the handle can be made from matching yarn.

5 Card Loom Weaving

Card loom weaving introduces a rigid type of loom. The cards are useful for making small articles, such as purses, mats, etc. Items such as tea cosies and slipper tops can be made by varying the shape of the loom, so that the finished piece of material is exactly the right size and shape for the particular project.

Through card loom weaving you can explore the possibilities of colour and weave variation, and it is a very good way of getting children started on the adventure of weaving. Incidentally card loom weaving should not be confused with card (or tablet) weaving, where the warp threads are passed through a series of cards with holes in each corner and are twisted to make the pattern. This type of weaving is not included in this book since, though it takes a minimal amount of equipment, it is very difficult to master without face-to-face tuition and needs a great deal of concentration and patience in order to achieve a worthwhile result.

The materials needed for card loom weaving can probably be found around the house.

a Good strong cardboard. Old cardboard boxes or packing are good, but if the cardboard is not thick enough to withstand threads being stretched over it without breaking or bending, you will need to thicken it by glueing several layers together.

b A sharp knife to cut the card, and ruler to measure it and then help to cut it straight. A pair of compasses is useful to make the round shapes.

c Yarn. You can begin by using up odd scraps of knitting wool. Handspun wool can also be used to add textural interest. Any thickness of yarn can be used, depending on how the card is cut and what you want to make. I would suggest starting with a 4-ply or double knitting wool.

d A needle to thread the weft thread in and out of the warp threads. A large blunt tapestry needle or bodkin is good, but if you have a weaving needle with a bent end, that is better. This can be made by bending a piece of wire to the shape shown in figure 19.

MAKING THE CARDS

Some card looms can be used many times, some are left inside the finished articles and some are torn away after the items have been woven.

Square and oblong cards can be used over and over again. Cut the card about 20 x 15 cm (8 x 6 in), or a square about 15 x 15 cm (6 x 6 in). Then cut notches along each end, about two notches per 1 cm (¼ in) apart. When the loom is threaded up, the yarn lies one thread in each notch to keep it evenly spaced, so make sure

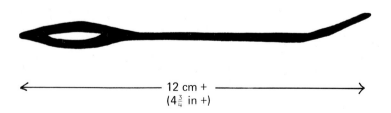

←———— 12 cm + ————→
(4¾ in +)

Figure 19 Weaving needle

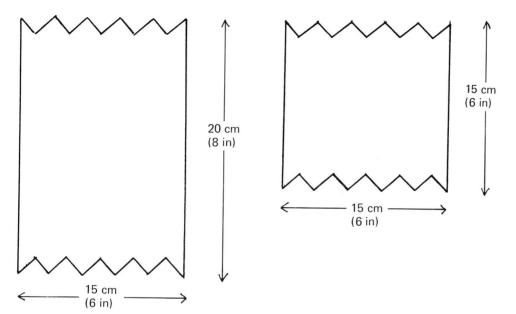

Figure 20 Oblong and square card looms

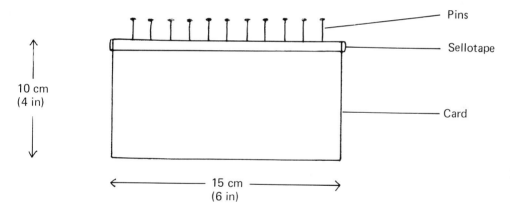

Figure 21 Card loom for a woven purse

that the notches are cut as accurately as possible.

There is a special card you can make for weaving a small purse. This needs very thick card, as ordinary sewing pins are stuck into one end to support the threads. You can use two pieces of card to make it even thicker, and if you put sticky tape over one end, it will help support the pins. The pins must be evenly spaced, again at about two pins per 1 cm (¼ in) apart, but if you intend to use a very fine yarn, then the pins could be a little closer.

If you want to make little mats, then the card will form an integral part of the finished article. It keeps the mat stiff and gives some protection to the table. Round mat cards for making these mats can be about 10 or 15 cm (4 or 6 in) diameter. Notches should again be cut around the outside of the card, about one per 1 cm (every ½ inch). You will also need to cut a 3 cm

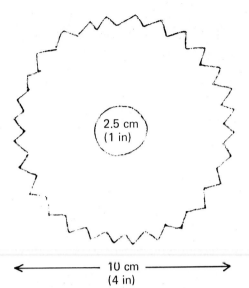

Figure 22 Round card loom

← ——— 10 cm ——— →
(4 in)

SETTING UP AND WEAVING ON THE CARDS

There are several ways of setting up the square and oblong cards. The first way uses just one side of the card. Tie a loop on the end of your warp thread and slip it on to the top left hand point of the card so that it is secure, as shown in figure 23. Then wind the yarn down and around the bottom point on the left, bringing it back on to the same side of the card. Bring the yarn up to the top again, pass it through the next free notch, then around and down, each time bringing the yarn back to the front side of the card. Continue this sequence until the card is covered with a series of parallel lines of thread. Tie the last thread to make it secure or tape it to the back of the card with sticky tape; the two ends can later be darned into the finished piece of weaving. The loom is now set and is ready for use.

You can also use both sides of the card, by winding the warp yarn around and around the card, moving over the card one notch at a time. Because of the notches, it is not possible to weave any longer length by using this method, but you will be able to weave both sides separately with only one lot of setting up, thus ending up with two similar shaped pieces, possibly for the two sides of a pin cushion, for example.

The purse card can be used over and over again. The warp thread is first tied to the pin on the extreme left. Then wind the yarn down and around the card, coming up around the same pin on the opposite side. Then take the thread down and behind the card, and up in front and around the second pin. Continue this sequence until the card is covered, and each pin has two threads going around it in opposite directions. Knot the thread around the last pin to finish off. The weaving is done around and around the card so that at the end the pins are removed and the purse is complete except for a

(1 in) diameter hole out of the centre of the card, as the warp threads are passed through the outer notches and then through this central hole.

You can make special cards to do specially shaped projects. A tea cosy card, for example, can be made by marking out a half spherical shape on the card. Detailed instructions for making and using this and other special cards will be found later in the chapter.

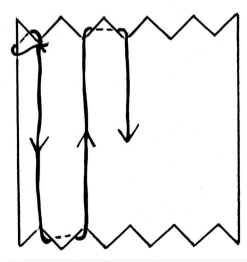

Figure 23 Threading up of square card loom

fastening at the top.

For the round mat cards, using the central hole and the notches, first stick the end of the yarn to the card to secure it temporarily, then take the yarn out and around the nearest notch. Continue winding, over the back of the card, up through the central hole and back out to the next notch. Note that the ball of wool you use will have to be small enough to pass easily through the central hole. Continue winding around and around until the whole card has been covered and finish off the loose end by tying it to the beginning thread.

Weaving on the cards involves the use of another thread (weft thread) and a needle or bodkin. This weft thread can be textured and a hand-spun yarn would be ideal for any of these projects. First try weaving a square card. Taking a fairly long length of yarn, begin at the bottom on the right and start weaving this thread in and out, over the first thread and under the second (as in darning). The loose end at the beginning can be darned in later, so leave a short length sticking out to make it easy. Push the first weft row down towards the bottom, making sure that it is even and not too taut. For the second row, from left to right, reverse the procedure and for every thread that you went over in the first row go under it in the second and vice versa (like bricks in a wall). When completed, push this row down hard up against the previous row, so that the fabric is nice and dense without any holes!

Tension is important. The weft thread should not be pulled so tight that the selvedges become indented. This you will get the feel of with practice, but for now be careful to pass the weft thread closely around the edge warp thread, but not too tightly so that it is pulled in.

On the square and oblong cards, keep on weaving to as near the top as

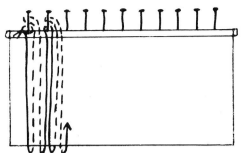

Figure 24 Threading up of purse card loom

you can. You will find that as you near the top it becomes more and more difficult to pass the needle through, but go on as long as you can. If you have wound the yarn on both sides of the card, then weave up the reverse side as above. When the weaving is completed, neaten the raw edges top and bottom by oversewing the ends and then cut the warp threads as near the top and bottom as possible. If you do not want the ends oversewn, then they can be hemstitched after the weaving has been cut off the loom.

For the purse cards, instead of weaving from side to side, weave around and around. Start at the bottom and push the first row threads down as hard as possible, so that when the purse is removed from the card there is no gap left at the bottom. When you have completed this row, turn the card over and continue weaving right to left on

Figure 25 Threading up of round card loom

the second side, and continue weaving around and around (one row alternately on each side) until you reach the top. To remove the completed purse, simply pull out the pins and take out the card. The purse is complete without the need for sewing any seams — just put some kind of fastening along the top and it will be ready for use.

For the round cards, start weaving at the centre and continue going around and around until you reach the outer edge of the card. The card is left inside the mat as a stiffener, so weave both sides of the card to complete the mat. Incidentally if you have an even number of warp threads, you will have to go over two at one point in order that the yarn is alternately over and under on the following rows. If you intend to make a set of mats, then I suggest you cut all the cards at one time, making sure that the same thickness of card is used for all the mats, and that they are all the same size.

WEAVE VARIATIONS

For the warp on the cards it is easiest to stick to one colour, as the warp is made from one continuous thread. Using more than one thread necessitates a knot at each colour change and if you are not very careful, they will show up in the finished piece.

In the weft there are many different variations that are possible to make your work more interesting. Colour is the most obvious one, using different yarns to create different coloured stripes across the fabric. These can be in regular or irregular designs. Use as few or as many different colours as you like and you will see the tremendous variety of effects which can be created.

Add some texture with your hand-spun wool to give card weaving another new dimension. Looped yarns, gimps and rough spun yarns all have their own particular characteristics which, if used carefully, will enhance your weaving. When using different

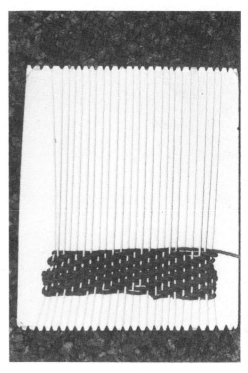

Photograph 11
Plain weave (left)

Photograph 12
Twill weave (right)

34

yarns, try to be aware of the purpose for which the weaving is to be designed. For a bag or purse you can use a variety of textured yarns, but a table mat needs to be fairly flat. To introduce a little stiffness in the finished article, try using raffia or even strips of cane.

Different thicknesses of yarn also add variety. Try a thin yarn and see how the rows will pack down tightly and obliterate the warp. A thick yarn is much quicker to weave and lets the warp threads show through as an integral part of the design.

In addition to this, there is the possibility of introducing variation in the weave itself. So far only plain weave (darning) has been mentioned. Basket weave goes over two threads and under two threads. Twill goes over two and under two, but at each row the pattern steps along one thread, thus giving a diagonal effect. You will find with these weaves that when you come to beat each row down, less of the warp threads will show in the finished weaving, compared to the same yarn used with plain weave.

There are many different variations possible, just by going over and under different numbers of threads and in different sequences. However, beware of letting the weft thread go over too many warps, as you will be left with long loops (floats) of yarn which (depending on the use of the finished piece) may either get easily pulled out and broken or may just look rather floppy!

As you can see there are endless possibilities and the best way to find them is to experiment.

SPECIAL PROJECTS

These projects involve the use of the third group of card looms mentioned above. The card is made specifically for a particular project and is cut or torn away once the weaving is finished. By using this method you can create a particular shape for a particular item.

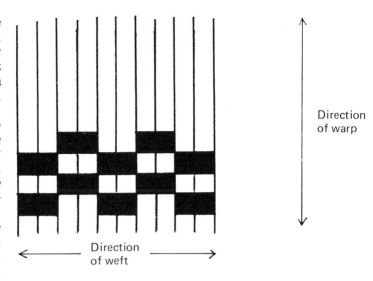

Figure 26 Basket weave

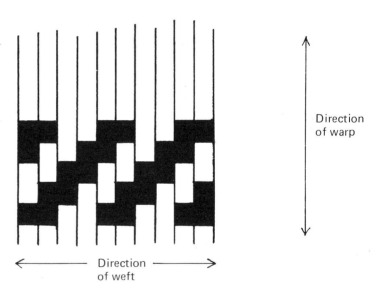

Figure 27 Twill weave

Mittens

The two mittens need to be exactly the same size and shape, so first of all lightly stick together two pieces of card on top of one another with sticky tape, so that when the holes for the yarn are

35

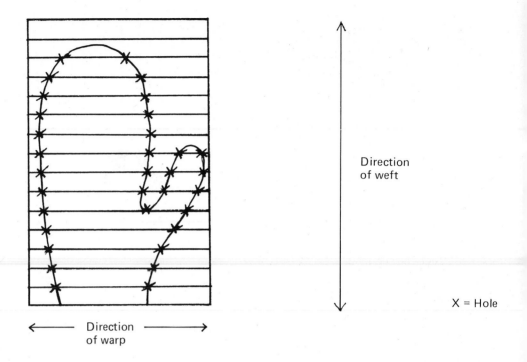

Direction
of weft

X = Hole

Direction
of warp

Figure 28 Card
loom for a woven
mitten

punched through the cards, the two
hands are exact. The card must be large
enough for each mitten. Place one of
your hands palm down on the top
card and draw around it with a pen.
To determine the finished size of the
mitten add at least 1.5 cm (½ in) all
around, and extend the mitten at the
bottom so that it will cover the wrist.
Then measure and draw parallel lines
across the card at about 1 cm (¼ in)
intervals; these grid lines enable the
warp threads to be evenly placed on
the mitten.

With a very sharp point, punch holes
around the outside of the mitten, at
each point where a grid line crosses it.
It is just as well to have a good pile of
old newspapers underneath while you
are making the holes, as the point must
go through both layers of card. When
the holes have been punched, separate
the two cards and weave each one as
described below.

Use about a double knitting wool
thickness. Thread a long piece of yarn
through a large blunt needle (tapestry
or knitter's needle) and starting at the
bottom of the mitten, thread the yarn
through each hole, winding it around
and around the card over the shape of
the mitten. Tie the starting yarn back
on to itself to secure. Where you have
to join another warp yarn, tie this as
neatly as possible to the previous
length. When you get up to where the
thumb joins, wind the yarn around
and around the thumb, knot it off at
the top and then go back and wind up
around the main part of the mitten.
The knots in the warp will get covered
in the weaving. Warp up the second
mitten in exactly the same way.

The finished mitten should have a
dense weave, so I would recommend
that, unless the weft yarn packs down
very closely, you use a twill weave.
Begin at the edge furthest away from
the thumb and weave from top to
bottom of the mitten, making sure
that the yarn is firmly packed down
as you go along.

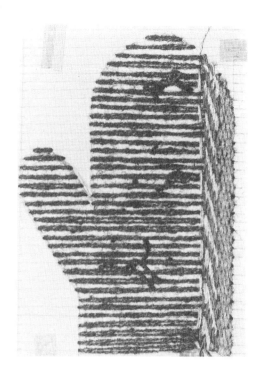

Photograph 13 Card loom mitten

Weave both sides of the mitten, and when the weaving is completed right up to the end of the thumb, tear away the cardboard and you should be left with the finished mitten, ready to wear with no sewing (except for darning in any loose ends). Weave the second mitten in exactly the same way.

Beret
With a pair of compasses, draw two circles on the card, both circles having the same centre. The smaller circle must fit your head measurement, adding about 2.5 cm (1 in) extra to allow for ease and shrinkage during weaving. Draw the outer circle however large you want the finished beret to be.

To punch the holes, use a ruler and pivotting this at the centre mark, punch one hole on each side of both circles, so that the holes are exactly opposite each other (four holes in one line). Rotate the ruler a little and punch four more holes. Do this until there are

holes all around the circles at regular intervals.

The threading up of this loom is slightly more complicated, as the card is woven differently on each side. The top of the beret is woven on the underside of the card, while the band and underside of the beret is woven on the top. Start by threading the yarn up one of the holes on the inner circle, back down the next adjacent hole and tie it

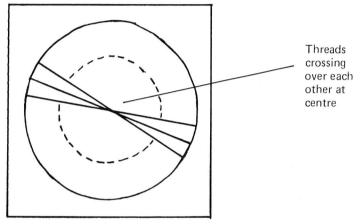

Figure 29 Card loom for a woven beret (top of beret)

Threads crossing over each other at centre

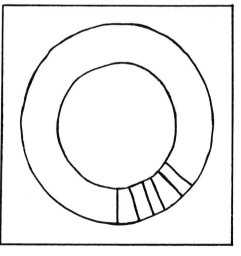

Figure 30 Card loom for a woven beret (underside of beret)

Figure 31 Side view of beret card loom

37

off to secure the end. Then, with the thread still on top of the card, take it over to the nearest hole in the outer circle and take it down to the reverse side of the card. The thread then crosses over the whole beret to the hole on the outer circle diagonally opposite and passes up to the top side of the card. Then take the thread through the nearest hole on the inner circle and back on top via the next adjacent hole. Take it back to the bottom of the card by the nearest hole in the outer circle. This time the thread should cross over the first thread on the bottom and come up through the hole in the outer circle diametrically opposite it. Continue threading like this until all the holes are used and then tie the end thread to the starting end.

When you have finished warping, add one extra thread from the outer circle to the middle on both back and front, so that there is an uneven number of threads in each complete circle of warp — if you do not do this you will find that the plain weave sequence will not work properly, as each thread must pass over and under alternately in each circle of weft.

To weave the beret, start at the middle on the top side of the beret and weave around and around until the whole of the large circle is completely woven. For the underneath of the beret, weave on the other side of the

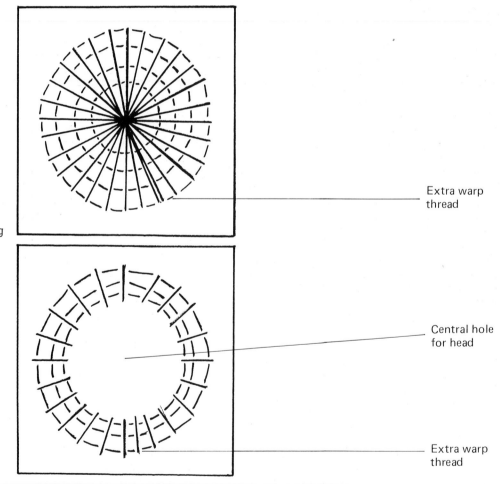

Figure 32 Top of beret card showing direction of weaving

Extra warp thread

Central hole for head

Figure 33 Bottom of beret card showing direction of weaving

Extra warp thread

card, from the inner circle to the outer circle.

Tear the card away when you have finished both sides and you should be left with the completed beret ready to wear!

Tea cosy

This shape and method can also be used to make a handbag or a round purse, etc. First of all, get a piece of cardboard large enough to trace on it the actual size of the tea cosy you want. Use an existing tea cosy or a pair of compasses to draw the shape you want (half a circle). Punch holes at even intervals round the edge of the circle to take the warp threads.

There is a problem in this design, namely that of holding the warp threads in place, so that the weft is woven in semi-circles around a central point. Some instructions say that you must use a ring on both sides in the centre at the bottom, but, as these rings have to stay in and form part of the finished design, the method outlined below avoids the need for these rings.

Instead of the ring, two anchor threads are stitched through the card over the bottom warp thread on each side — at 'B' and 'C' in figure 34. Use a thread different to the warp yarn, punch a hole in the card at both 'B' and 'C', and insert an anchor thread through the holes at both points, tying it securely in place. Note that the bottom warp thread is not level with the bottom line. This is important as the weaving should straighten out when the cord is removed at the end. This loop of thread acts like the ring described above, but has the advantage of not showing in the finished work.

Now using this thread to support one end of the warp threads and the holes on the outside of the circle to support the others, set up the card ready for weaving as follows. Starting

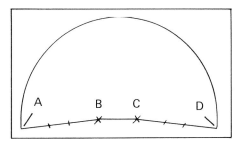

Figure 34 Tea cosy card showing first warp thread

on the front of the card, tie the first warp thread to the loop between 'B' and 'C', take this thread out and thread it through the hole at 'A'. Then pass the thread over the reverse of the card to the loop 'B' to 'C' on the reverse, thread the yarn around this loop and take it back to the outside of the circle to the next hole to 'A' and so up to the front of the card again. Continue this all around the card until it has been threaded right round on both sides.

It is a good idea at this stage to put a few stitches through the cord and over the bottom warp thread between 'A' and 'B', and 'C' and 'D'. This helps to keep this thread in place as there is a tendency for it to pull in while weaving.

To weave, start at the centre and weave in half-circles until the outside edge is reached. Make sure you weave both sides, before removing the anchor thread and tearing away the card.

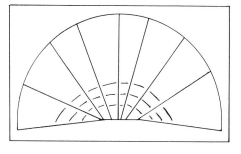

Figure 35 Tea cosy card showing direction of warp and weft threads

6 Using a Frame Loom

Up to now we have used first the body (finger weaving) and then pieces of cardboard (card loom weaving) on which to support the warp threads for weaving. In this chapter we will explore the possibilities of using a frame on which to weave. This has several advantages. One is that you can make the frame whatever size you like — a small one if you want to be able to carry it around and pick up the work at odd moments, or a very large one if you are interested in weaving on a large scale.

There are two different types of work which are possible on a frame loom: free weaving and tapestry weaving. In practice they can be mixed together, but I have distinguished them as they have rather different characteristics.

Using these techniques, it is possible to be much freer in the weaving compared to finger weaving and card loom weaving, and to introduce all kinds of different materials into woven hangings. The frame can of course be used over and over again.

MAKING THE FRAME

If you are not very good at woodwork, or perhaps just want to quickly try out this type of weaving, then there are several different items that can be utilized.

On a very small scale, the polystyrene dishes that you sometimes get with meat or vegetables in supermarkets are ideal. The threads can be wrapped around and around the dish, and woven with the dish the right way up, so there is plenty of room to move the needle up and down inside the dish itself. This is a good size on which to experiment with some of the different techniques described below.

A picture frame is the next best idea. The size does not matter, but the frame should be reasonably flat (not one with decorative mouldings) and strong. It must be strong because of the tension put on the warp threads while weaving.

Ideally a purpose-built frame is best, and you can make it whatever size you like. The one for which I give details is about 40 cm (16 in) square, as I think that this is a fairly good size on which to start. If you want to make a larger

Photograph 14 Frame weaving on small polystyrene dish

Photograph 15
Frame weaving, by
Joan Ward

one, then use correspondingly thicker wood, as the larger it is the more tension is exerted on it by the yarn and also the wood may be liable to twist.

Figure 36 is fairly self-explanatory, but here are a few suggestions. The wood used must be strong and the edges should be well sanded, so that threads do not catch on any rough splinters. The corners of the frame can be placed on top of one another and glued and nailed. The most important thing is to make a very firm joint, so the frame is rigid and the sides are at right angles to each other. If you can mitre the corners (as in a picture frame), this makes a much neater looking job, but it is not necessary from a practical point of view. If the wood on the top and bottom bars is slightly angled, it facilitates rolling the warp around the frame.

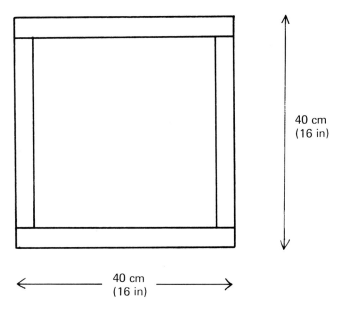

40 cm
(16 in)

40 cm
(16 in)

Figure 36 Frame for frame loom weaving

41

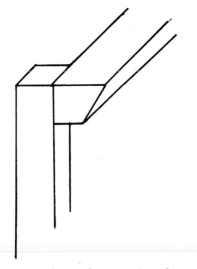

Figure 37 Side view of corner of frame

Some ready-made weaving frames you see may have either notches in the top and bottom bars, or nails spaced at regular intervals along them. These methods are used to space the warp threads evenly. This is fine if you are going to stick to using one thickness of warp yarn. If, as I hope, after you have read this book, you want to experiment with all different kinds of yarn, you will probably find nails or notches rather restricting. Outlined below is a method of spacing the warp on the loom, which does not necessitate the use of either of these devices.

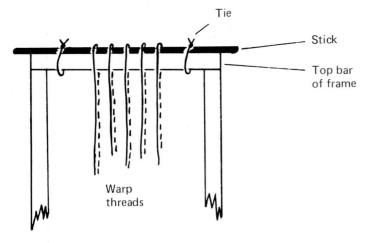

Figure 38 Tension stick tied to top bar of frame

WARPING THE FRAME

There are several different methods of warping, depending on what you want to weave and how you want to control the tension on the frame.

The simplest method is to wind the yarn around and around the frame over both top and bottom bars, starting at one side and working gradually over to the other. Winding the yarn around is easy, but it means you have very little control over the tension as you weave. Wind as loosely as possible, because as you weave the warp threads will inevitably tighten up — and then you will find out if your frame is really strong enough! If the warp gets too tight, you will also find it very difficult to pull it around the frame as you weave. The simplest way to help overcome this problem is to tie a stick over the top and/or bottom bar of the frame before you start warping. Then if you find the warp yarn getting too tight as you weave, just untie the stick and slip it out from under the warp threads and this will loosen the overall tension a little.

There is a more complicated way of controlling tension involving the use of two sticks, which is recommended if you are thinking of working on a large scale. The two sticks should be tied parallel to each other, so that there is a gap between them. Then tie them on to the frame, so that they are held in position about half way up one side. If you drill a hole at each end of the sticks, the ties will be prevented from slipping out of place while you are warping the frame.

Now wind the warp yarn on to the frame, but this time a little differently from the method described above. Secure the first warp end to the upper stick, then pass it up and over the top bar, down the length of the back of the frame, and bring it up under the bottom bar to the bottom stick. Wind the yarn around the bottom stick and take it down around the bottom bar,

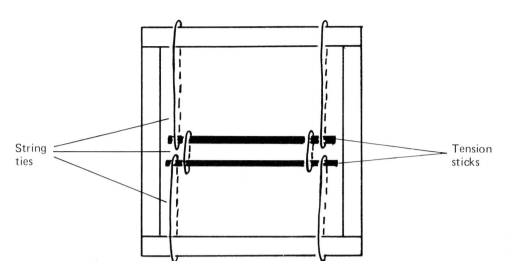

String ties

Tension sticks

Figure 39 Tension sticks tied in position on frame

up to the top bar, and down to the top stick. Continue this sequence until you have as many warp threads as you need, making sure that no warp threads cross the short gap between the two tension sticks. The long outer ties should be removed before weaving, as their only function is to hold the sticks in place while setting up the warp.

As the warp gets tighter during the weaving process, all you do is untie the strings between the two tension sticks and increase the gap between them slightly before retying. Using this method you can keep control over the tension as the work progresses. Incidentally if you are working on a large scale or if the sticks are not strong enough, they will tend to bow in the middle. This problem can be alleviated by inserting more ties between the tension sticks.

Both of the above methods of warping assume that you want to weave an area of nearly twice the frame size — that is both back and front of the frame. If you want to weave a hanging the size of the frame only, it would be rather wasteful to wind the threads all the way around, and then to discard half the warp when the finished work is cut off the frame. To weave only one

side, wind the warp threads around the frame, but this time in a figure of eight. Ignore the cross in the threads when you weave, and thus you will not

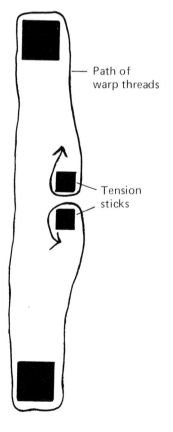

Path of warp threads

Tension sticks

Figure 40 Side view of frame, showing path of warp with two tension sticks

43

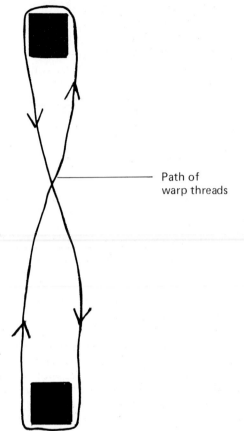

Figure 41 Side view of frame showing path of warp with figure of eight

wool is not strong enough to withstand the stresses and strains put upon it when weaving. A strong cotton weaving yarn is best, but if you have any odd balls of crochet or dishcloth cotton, they are fine to begin with. A smooth string is also good for tapestry weaving, but to start with do not use anything too fine.

How many threads should you wind on the frame? Start off by deciding how wide you want the finished piece to be and then add at least an extra 5 cm (2 in) to allow for shrinkage during weaving. You do not of course have to use the entire width of the frame for every project, but in any case do not wind the yarn so close to the edges that it is liable to fall off the frame. Next work out how many threads per 5 cm (2 in) you will need. This of course depends on the warp and weft yarns you intend to use, but for a medium thickness string try about eight or ten threads per 5 cm (four or five per 1 in). If you find that when you weave, the warp is being hidden more than you wanted, put more threads in the same width next time, or if too little of the weft is visible, then use fewer threads per 5 cm (2 in). Knowing how many threads to use in a given width is really a matter of trial and error at first, until you achieve the finished effect you desire.

To space the warp evenly once it is wound around the loom (without the use of nails or notches) you need to use a spacer thread. There are several methods of doing this, but the simplest involves twisting a spacer thread around each warp thread, in order to separate it from the threads on either side. Take a long length of string (about three times the width of your frame) and fold it in half to find the mid-point. Starting at the left hand side of the frame, place half of the spacer thread in front of the warp and the other half behind, with the mid-point of the string around the left bar of the frame near

waste more than necessary of the warp yarn.

Up to now it has not been mentioned what yarn to use for the warp. Of course it depends on what you want to make, but whatever you do use, it must be strong and smooth in texture. You may find that your handspun

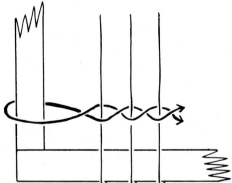

Figure 42 Spacing the warp threads on the frame

44

the bottom. Then pull the string from behind to the front and push the front string to the back, forming a cross in the string. Do the same between the first and second warp threads, pulling the thread from the back forward and pushing the front string back. Continue to do this between each warp thread all along the width of the warp, and when you reach the right hand side, tie the spacer string loosely around the right hand side of the frame. Every warp thread should now be separated from the other two next to it by a cross in the string. (Incidentally, after having woven several inches, the spacer thread can be removed, so that the weaving can be pulled around the frame.)

When you begin to weave, it is easiest to keep the first few rows of weft straight, if you can beat them up against a hard edge. Use a smooth, flat stick or a ruler, and thread this under and over each alternate warp thread. Then push the stick as far down towards the bottom of the frame as you can, so that it lies hard up against the spacer thread. Having done this, you are now ready to weave on the frame.

TECHNIQUES FOR WEAVING

This section is divided into two parts. Free weaving is a much more loosely defined technique and the free use of techniques and materials means that interesting textural effects can be created. Tapestry weaving is essentially a very flat and even technique. Both techniques can be used to create interesting wall hangings, while tapestry woven fabric also makes good strong bags or mats. In some cases, both techniques can be used in the same piece of weaving.

Tapestry weaving

First of all, a note about the word 'tapestry'. This should not be confused with canvas work (sometimes known as needlework tapestry). With canvas work a ready-woven canvas is used and the yarn is stitched through it in such a way as to cover the canvas completely, so that it is not visible in the finished work. The word 'tapestry' used only to refer to woven tapestry, but it has crept into the needleworker's vocabulary over the years. True tapestry is woven, and if you look at old tapestries in country houses, you will see that they are usually woven, the large thick panels being used to cover damp and draughty walls. With woven tapestry, the warp threads are completely hidden by the weft (the reverse of finger weaving), but unlike canvas work, the background threads are held together by the finished tapestry. It is rather clumsy to keep on writing 'woven tapestry' every time, so whenever you see the word 'tapestry' written in this book, it automatically refers to woven tapestry.

It was mentioned above that tapestry is a weft-faced fabric. The warp for this must therefore be spaced wide enough apart, so that the weft yarns can be packed down tightly together. The best way to beat them down is to use an old fork. If you still find that the warp shows, then either use a thinner weft thread or space the warp threads further apart (or go under two and over two at a time). Use a strong yarn for the warp, either cotton or linen or a fine string, provided it is smooth and fairly tightly spun. Set the warp yarn at about ten or twelve threads per 5 cm (five or six threads per 1 in).

The weft yarn you use should be smooth, and you may need a good variety of colours if you want to create a picture. The yarn does not need to be soft, and in fact a fairly hard yarn is better, as it will make a firmer tapestry. Carpet wool is ideal (the 2-ply kind as used in the machine weaving of carpets) and if you have a local carpet factory, you may be able to buy ends of warps fairly cheaply.

These ends are known as 'thrums', and provided you do not mind sorting them out, you can get a good variety of colours in short and long lengths. If you use your handspun wool, you will need a good variety of natural and/or dyed colours before you start.

To thread the weft through, use a weaving needle or bodkin for the short lengths. A blunt needle with a bent end is ideal, and if you can get or make a long one of about 25 cm (10 in), it helps to accelerate the weaving process. You can make one by bending some strong wire into the shape shown in figure 19. You will need one needle for each colour but, where there are a number of colours being woven in one row, you can just thread them through with your fingers, and use the fork to beat the yarn down into place.

If you are serious about doing tapestry weaving, it is best to get or make some wooden tapestry bobbins, as shown in figure 43. These are round and really need to be turned on a lathe. The yarn is wound around and around the narrow shaft of the bobbin, and the point on the end is used (instead of the fork) to beat the weft. Again, you really need one of these for each colour used.

Up until now, we have only used one colour of weft thread along each line. In tapestry weaving, this rule is broken in order to create pictures from the yarn. The simple techniques using plain weave are described below.

One point is worth making before you start: if you are going to hang your tapestry on the wall, it is better to weave it sideways, as it will hang better. Old tapestries were designed to cover the bare stone walls of houses and castles, and if you get the chance to examine any of these closely, you will find that most of them were woven sideways (with the warp going across the finished design).

Weaving a picture

Start by deciding on your design. Begin with something simple, such as a few abstract shapes. When you have mastered the basic skills, you can go on to more figurative work (a picture of your house or garden for example). If you are good at artwork, make your own original drawings, or otherwise use a photograph, either your own or one from a glossy magazine. My own personal favourite is to translate well known paintings into tapestry, using coloured plates from books or calendars, as this satisfies my other interest in art history at the same time. The possibilities are endless.

When you have decided on the subject, you should make a full-size pattern (cartoon) of the design on paper. Mark in the most important lines and give some indication of the colours, possibly using a watercolour

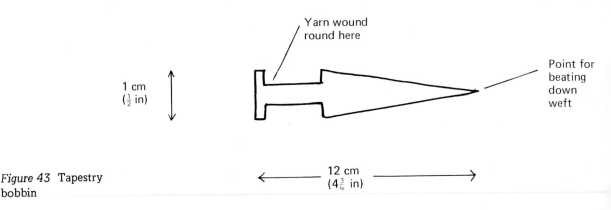

Yarn wound round here

Point for beating down weft

1 cm ($\frac{1}{2}$ in)

12 cm ($4\frac{3}{4}$ in)

Figure 43 Tapestry bobbin

46

wash. When you have warped the frame, sellotape the cartoon on to the back of the frame, so that the design is visible through the warp threads. Use this as a guide when you are working, in order to know what shapes to weave and when to change colour.

Start weaving at the bottom of the frame, after inserting the spacer thread and stick, as described in the previous section. Leave the ends of the weft threads hanging loose in front of the weaving, since the front will end up as the reverse side of the tapestry. The completed tapestry will be a mirror image of the cartoon, so bear this in mind when drawing out your design.

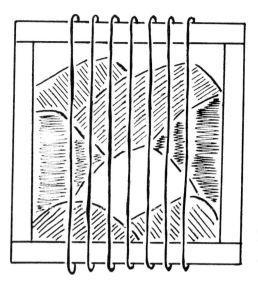

Figure 44 Tapestry design attached behind warp threads on the frame

Photograph 16 Tapestry technique

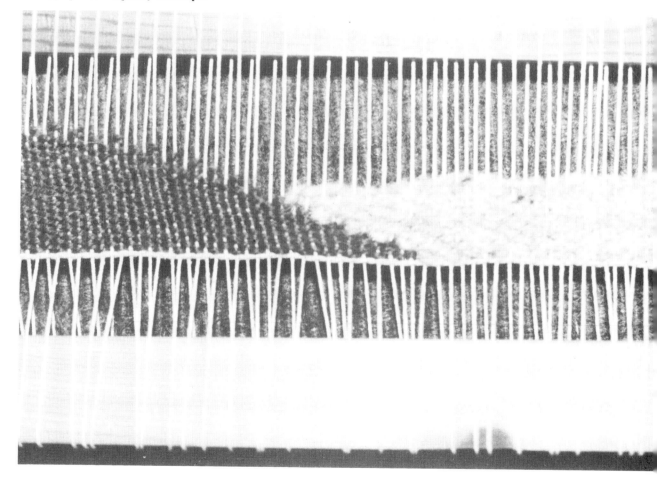

47

Figure 45 Order of
weaving colour
tapestry blocks

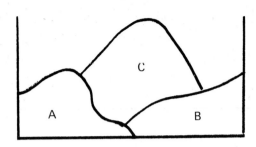

Weaving tapestry by this method is a little like painting by numbers! Start at one corner and using colour 'A', fill in the first shape, using the cartoon as a guide and weaving in plain weave. Remember to beat up the weft threads as hard as you can after each row, so that there are no holes left in the design and no sign of the warp threads. Disregard the remainder of the warp where colour 'A' does not appear and build up the yarn into the shape you want.

Next do the same with colour 'B' and then colour 'C'. You will find that there is a slit which appears where the colours join. This can be left as part of the finished effect, sewn up when the work is removed from the frame or there are various methods for overcoming the problem, which will be explained in the next section.

Continue to build up the colours until the design is finished. However,

where one colour overlaps another colour, weave in the order shown in figure 46. You would find that if you wove sections 1 and 3 together, it would be very difficult to join in colour 'A' between 'X' and 'Y' as marked on the diagram.

When you have completed the design, cut the tapestry off the frame. The loose warp ends can be knotted into a fringe (if this is to form part of the finished visible design) or sewn back into the tapestry (so they are hidden from view). Either hang the tapestry on sticks top and bottom, or get it blocked, mounted and framed.

Tapestry techniques

Methods to deal with the slits as mentioned above are as follows:

a Leave the slits in the work and sew them up when the tapestry has been removed from the frame.

b If you weave the colours up row by row (that is working all the colours in one row before proceeding to the next row), use either this or the next method of linking the threads together. Figure 47 shows how the colours are twisted around each other between the weft threads.

c Overlapping the threads of each colour around the same warp thread means that vertical slits are avoided, but this method may provide a rather more bulky join, especially where there is a long straight vertical slit to cover.

As well as hangings, pieces of tapestry make good strong bags, though it is probably better to line them inside, rather than trying to darn in all the loose weft ends at the back. A cord for the handle of the bag can be made in matching yarn, such as from the inkle bands described in the next chapter.

Any of these tapestry techniques can also be incorporated into free weaving.

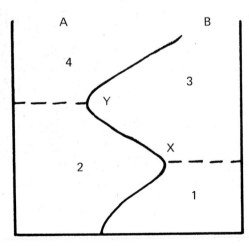

Figure 46 Order of
weaving irregular
shaped colour
tapestry blocks

1 Samples of dyed wool mounted on card

2 Skeins of dyed and natural wool

3 Detail of handwoven cushion in handspun wool (natural white, natural black and red dyed with cochineal) by Evelyn Green

4 Fingerwoven belts

Photograph 17 Tapestry (woven sideways) from a painting by Van Gogh, woven by Jennifer Green

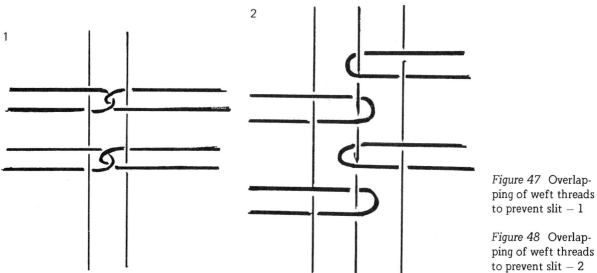

Figure 47 Overlapping of weft threads to prevent slit — 1

Figure 48 Overlapping of weft threads to prevent slit — 2

49

Free weaving

Free weaving presents a much more flexible approach to weaving hangings, both in the techniques and the use of materials. I think it is important to try the technically more skilled methods of tapestry weaving, but once these techniques have been mastered, there are many fascinating ways you can experiment.

The materials you can use are as varied as the ways of interpreting the design. Again, a string warp can be used, but this time you can either cover it completely (as in tapestry weaving) or leave parts of it exposed to form an integral part of the design. String, raffia and baling twine can all be used for weft, as can wool, cotton and manmade fibres. These materials can be mixed, as wall hangings are not usually washed, so that the different shrinkage rates of the various materials will not have any adverse effects.

Some of the rolags from your spinning can be inserted (it is better to wash them carefully first) and the warp threads will hold the loose fibres in place. Intersperse strips of cane with plain weave, and you can make very attractive table mats. Sticks and leaves from the garden give interesting textures, and beads or stones can be threaded on to the weft threads in order to hold them in place.

There is no need to weave in straight rows. Patches of colour and texture can be built up at random in order to create some fascinating abstract designs. Either make up a design before you begin, or experiment with textures and colours as you go along. One idea is to design a hanging on a theme such as a holiday, using found materials. Collect the things you will need for this when you go on holiday (for example, fleece from the hedgerows in the country, or shells and pebbles from the seaside, etc.) and when you get home and weave up the materials, you can create a unique souvenir of a happy time.

In addition to using the tapestry techniques described above and interesting fibres to create textural interest, there are also various other ways of creating interesting visual areas, some of which are obtained as follows:

a Raised pile texture. This involves

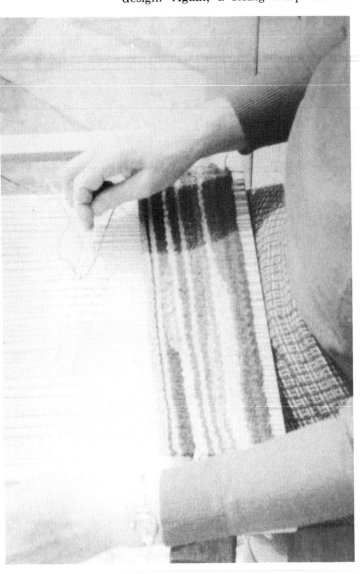

Photograph 18 Frame weaving, using needle to thread the weft thread in and out of the warp threads

50

the insertion in the warp of short lengths of yarn, in order to make a three-dimensional effect. Cut some short lengths of wool (to get them all the same length, wind them around a couple of rulers or two pieces of card). The length of these depends on how long you want the finished pile — if you just want a slightly raised surface, keep the lengths short, but for a decorative fringe effect, longer lengths can be used. Thread the lengths individually around two warp threads, as shown in figure 49. One row of these knots adds interest to the woven piece, or a whole area provides a richly textured surface.

b The technique known as 'soumak' creates a slightly raised surface very quickly. One weft thread is wrapped back on itself and around two warp threads as it is taken across the warp. This can also be reversed (left to right/ right to left), so that one row of each will produce a chain effect.

c There is no need to weave the whole of the hanging, and the use of gaps deliberately made can give an interesting effect. Several warp threads can be wrapped together and drawn in tightly. This technique can be very effective if the hanging is mounted or hung against a contrasting background, for example, a black hanging on a white wall.

There are many other ways of making interest and texture in your work, and the above ideas and the examples illustrated will help you to get started.

To finish off the hanging you can knot or oversew the ends, and tie the top and bottom on sticks. Stones suspended from the bottom of the warp will help give the hanging some weight if it tends to curl up when it is hung. An interesting idea for a very fine lightweight design is to mount it on to lampshade card, and create an original lampshade to match the colour scheme of your room. (Remember, however, that if the hanging is too densely woven, the light will not shine through it!)

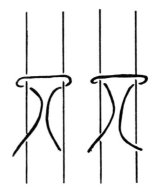

Figure 49 Pile weave

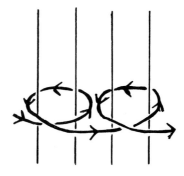

Figure 50 Looped weave

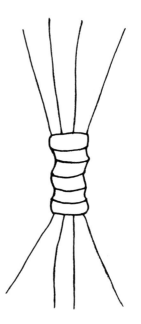

Figure 51 Wrapped warp threads

51

Photograph 19
String hanging, by
Jennifer Green

52

BOARD LOOM

So far in this chapter I have described tapestry and free weaving hangings, most of which are square or rectangular. Neither of these methods is suitable for making clothes, as it would be very difficult to cut the fabric without it fraying badly. However, there is a way of using a board loom to produce shaped weaving, so that you can weave the pieces of the garment exactly to fit.

You will need a good strong piece of board, one that is thick enough to hold nails upright and firmly in position. The size of the board depends on what you want to make, but it is better to have one that is too large, rather than be restricted in what you can weave.

Work out accurately on paper the shape you want to weave. The shape outlined in figure 52 is for half the front of a waistcoat. You can use a

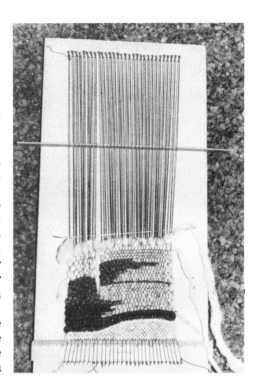

Photograph 20
Freeweaving on board loom

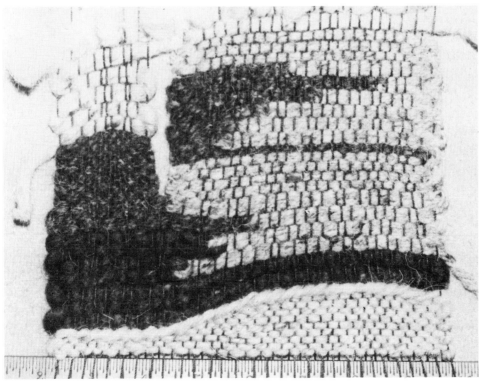

Photograph 21
Detail of freeweaving

53

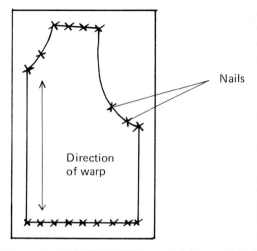

Direction
of warp

Nails

Figure 52 Board
loom

dressmaker's paper pattern for getting the right shape for clothes, but do remember to allow plenty of room for 'ease'.

Transfer this shape on to the board and knock in nails at top and bottom of the shape. These nails should be about 1 cm (½ in) apart and they are used to support the warp threads. The board must be thick enough to hold the nails firmly in place, even under the tension exerted by the warp threads.

Tie the warp thread to the nail at the bottom left hand corner, and wind it up around the nail at the top left corner. Bring this thread back down to the bottom row of nails and around the second nail from the left. Continue to wind the yarn up and down around the nails until the warp is complete, and tie the end around the last nail.

Weave the shape using a needle, as for card loom weaving, beginning at the bottom and working your way up to the top. Any of the tapestry or free weaving techniques can be used as described above, depending on the type of garment you want. If you want a very light, open fabric, then the garment may need to be lined when it is made up. Also if there are many loose ends, it may be best to line the garment. If the edges are not very neat when the weaving is taken off the board, you can oversew or bind the ones that show in the finished garment, though where the pieces are joined to each other in the seams there is obviously no need to do this.

Using this technique, which is rather like a combination of card loom weaving and frame loom weaving, you can design your own original clothes. For example, you can make a waistcoat with a tapestry picture on it, or using lurex create a loose open weave evening jacket. Ribbons can also be used as weft for a more decorative effect.

The possibilities are endless and this idea of shaped weaving can be extended to weave any shape you like, anything from egg cosies to coats!

7 Inkle Loom Weaving

The origin of the word 'inkle' is not known, but we can be certain that it is a very old form of weaving. Inkle weaving produces a warp-faced fabric, suitable for braids and bands. The width of the material is governed by the number of threads that will comfortably fit on to the pegs of the loom without falling off the ends, though it is possible to make a double-sided inkle loom, and then the pegs and the weaving can be much wider.

The warp for the inkle band is made on the loom, as the threads are wound around the pegs. Using this type of loom introduces two new devices to speed up the weaving process. Small loops of string (heddles) are made to separate alternate warp threads. Instead of having to weave the weft thread in and out with a needle, the heddles enable the weaver to separate the two sets of threads in order to form a gap (the shed) through which the weft thread can quickly be passed. The weft thread is wound around a wooden stick (shuttle) and weaving becomes much easier and quicker.

MAKING AN INKLE LOOM
Working drawings for making a table inkle loom are shown in figures 53

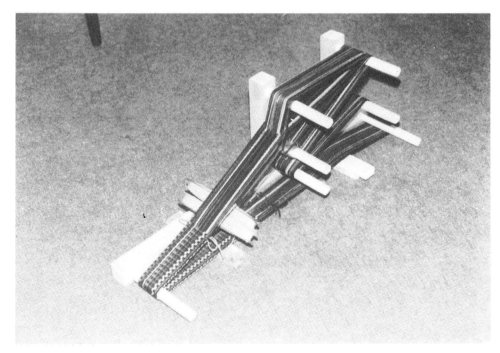

Photograph 22
Inkle loom

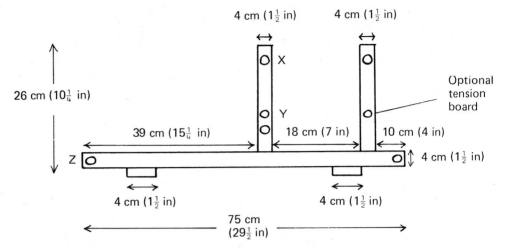

4 cm ($1\frac{1}{2}$ in)   4 cm ($1\frac{1}{2}$ in)

26 cm ($10\frac{1}{4}$ in)

X

Y

Optional tension board

39 cm ($15\frac{1}{4}$ in)   18 cm (7 in)   10 cm (4 in)

Z

4 cm ($1\frac{1}{2}$ in)

4 cm ($1\frac{1}{2}$ in)   4 cm ($1\frac{1}{2}$ in)

75 cm ($29\frac{1}{2}$ in)

Figure 53 Side view of inkle loom

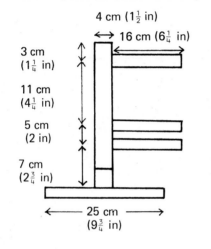

4 cm ($1\frac{1}{2}$ in)

16 cm ($6\frac{1}{4}$ in)

3 cm ($1\frac{1}{4}$ in)

11 cm ($4\frac{1}{4}$ in)

5 cm (2 in)

7 cm ($2\frac{3}{4}$ in)

25 cm ($9\frac{3}{4}$ in)

Figure 54 End view of inkle loom

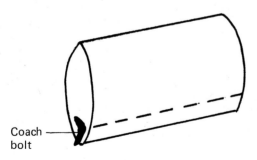

Coach bolt

Figure 55 Tension board for inkle loom

and 54. The main point to stress is that the loom must be strong and the pegs sturdy, since there is a lot of tension put on the pegs as the band is woven and pulled round the loom. Make sure that the pegs fit tightly into the holes and do not move when yarn is put around them under tension. A simple block of wood can be inserted for tension adjustment, but it is better to have a swivel board (as shown in figure 55) with a coach bolt to tighten and loosen it in order to adjust the angle of the board. This tension arm is made to swivel, so that the tension on the band can be tightened or loosened as required during weaving. As the band is woven, the warp tends to get tighter, so that the tension can be slackened using the tension bar. It is also necessary to slacken tension when winding the warp around the loom as the weaving progresses.

As well as the loom itself you will need at least one wooden stick shuttle on which to wind the weft yarn. Use strong wood and make the shuttle as thin as possible, so that it can be used to beat the weft threads into place as well. As with the loom itself, it is important to make sure that the wood is smooth and well sanded. Any rough edges may catch the wool and ruin your weaving.

The other equipment you need to make before you begin are the heddles. These are short loops of string and you will need half the number of these to the total number of warp threads you intend to use. Start by making about thirty, and do more as you need them — these heddles are used over and over again. A thin smooth string or linen thread is suitable for making the heddles, as they must not stretch while they are being used. In order to get all the heddles the same length, use the two pegs marked 'X' and 'Y' in figure 53. Place a length of string in a circle around these two pegs, and tie securely with a reef knot. Cut the ends and remove it from the loom. It is the use of these heddles that forms the space (shed) through which the shuttle passes when weaving.

THREADING THE LOOM

The most important principle to remember when threading the loom is that each alternate thread must pass through a heddle. If this does not happen you will find mistakes in the pattern, which are very difficult to put right once the weaving has started. The more carefully the loom is prepared, the better weaving will result.

For the first project, thread up the loom with alternate contrasting colours (one thread black, one thread white) so that any mistakes will be easy to spot. Once you have mastered this technique, go on and experiment with the colour and pattern variations described in the next section.

The yarn used for the warp should be smooth, otherwise it will tend to stick to itself and will be difficult to weave. Some oddments of knitting wool are good to begin with, say a 4-ply or double knitting. Cotton is also

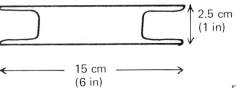

Figure 56 Stick shuttle

2.5 cm (1 in)

15 cm (6 in)

very good for bookmarks, bags, etc. Whatever yarn you use, you will need at least two different colours of the same weight, in order to form the pattern in the band. Inkle weaving is in some ways very similar to finger weaving in that it produces a warp-faced plain weave band, with the pattern being produced by colour variations.

In order to help thread up the loom, it is useful to hammer a large headed tack into the end of the loom which is nearest the weaver as you thread up ('Z' in figure 53). When you begin to thread, wind the yarn around this tack to hold it temporarily in place, until it is eventually tied to the other end of the circle of yarn.

To thread up, take the first white thread, wrap the end around the tack, pass it up towards the top back peg and on around the other pegs in sequence and back to the front, as shown in figure 57. Unwrap the end around the tack and tie this to the other end of the yarn, so that it forms one complete circle around the loom. Be careful not to wind the yarn full circle round any one of the pegs, because if you do, the warp will not pull round the loom as you weave. (Incidentally, if you have a tension board, make sure that this is extended outwards to at least 45 degrees, as the warp tends to get tighter as you weave. With a tension block, tie it to the back foot of the loom before you start to thread up and remove it when weaving if the warp gets too tight.)

Next take a black thread, wind it around the tack as before, but this

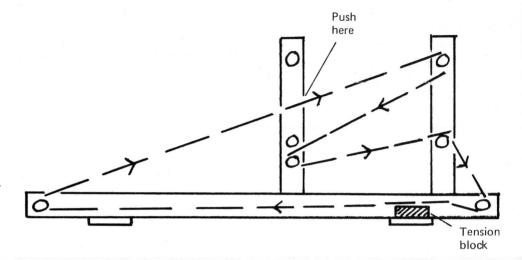

Figure 57 Thread-
ing up the inkle
loom — 1

Push
here

Tension
block

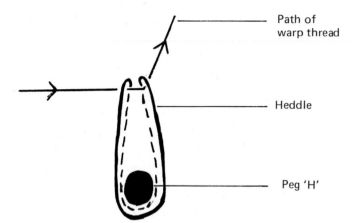

Path of
warp thread

Heddle

Peg 'H'

Figure 58 Inkle
loom heddle

time keep hold of the end in your left
hand. Take one string heddle and loop
it over peg 'H'. Pass the heddle over the
warp thread you are holding and then
loop the other end back on to peg 'H'
(figure 58). Then pass the black warp
thread over the top peg nearest to you
and then let it follow the same course
as the previous white thread, until it
comes full circle and can be tied back
on to itself.

Continue threading alternate white
and black threads (making sure that
each black thread passes through a

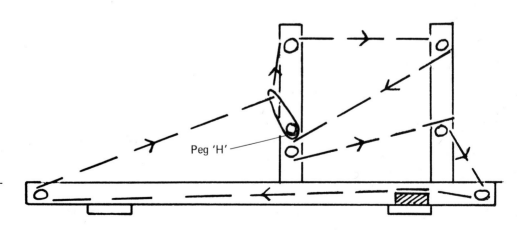

Peg 'H'

Figure 59 Thread-
ing up the inkle
loom — 2

heddle) until the band is as wide as will fit easily on the pegs. Note that if it is too wide, the yarn will tend to fall off the back pegs and the tension board while you are weaving.

Having threaded up the loom, you should be able to see that whereas up to the heddles the black and white threads are together, after the place where the heddles pull down the black threads there is a gap between the two different coloured threads. It is this gap that enables the weaver to make the space through which the shuttle will pass.

WEAVING ON THE INKLE LOOM
To obtain the two sheds necessary to get plain weave, first push the warp down with your right hand just behind the heddles, as shown in figure 57. You will find that when you do this, a gap appears between the two sets of threads near the weaver. The opposite set of threads can be pulled on top by gently putting your right hand under the white threads behind the heddles and lifting them up on top of the black threads.

As the inkle is a warp-faced band, the weft will show only at the edges of the finished band. If you do not want this to be obvious, use the same coloured yarn for the weft as the outer edge colour of the warp. Thus if, as above, you start and end with a white thread, use a white thread for weft and it will not show on the band.

Wind the weft yarn around a shuttle. If you put on plenty of yarn (enough to finish the band) then you will not have to join in new weft threads in the middle of the band. As in the other types of weaving, it is much easier to begin weaving if you can beat the first few rows of weft down against a hard edge. Cut two small pieces of card, about 15 cm (6 in) long by about 1 cm (½ in) wide, and insert them as the first two rows of your weaving.

Make the first shed as described above, by pushing down on the threads behind the heddles, insert the first piece of card and pull it down hard towards you. Make the second shed by lifting the same threads and insert the second card, pulling it down hard against the first piece. The third shed is the same as the first, but this time insert the first row of weft yarn. Leave the end of the yarn sticking out, as it can be sewn in later. Pull the yarn down hard against the card, using the shuttle as a beater. Change the shed and beat hard again with the edge of the shuttle. Insert the second weft thread and pull this in tight and hard, so that the warp threads are pulled tightly together and the first weft thread is not visible (remember you are trying to weave a warp-faced band). One of the advantages that the inkle band has over the finger woven band is that the inkle can produce a hard firm braid, firm enough to use as bag handles or guitar straps.

As you weave up towards the heddles, you will find the shed space becoming increasingly smaller. When it is too narrow for the shuttle to pass easily through without catching any of the warp threads accidentally, slacken off the tension if you can, and pull the whole band towards you. It should slip easily around the loom (remove the pieces of card if they do not easily go round). Pull the band so that the woven piece is showing for at least 2.5 cm (1 in) on top, tighten the tension again and continue weaving. Go on weaving as above and use as much of the warp as you can; you will find that at the end the shed becomes so small that the shuttle catches in the warp threads.

Cut the woven band off the loom, removing the heddles and keeping them safely to use again. Sew the loose weft ends at each end into the band, in order to stop the ends from unravelling. Cut the warp ends to form a neat fringe or hem each end, depending on how you intend to use the band.

Photograph 23 Weaving on the inkle loom

WEAVING WITH TWO SHUTTLES

This method is an alternative way of weaving to that described above. In using this method it is much easier to obtain even selvedges. You will need two wooden stick shuttles, each wound with weft yarn, as the two weft threads are passed in opposite directions through the same warp shed.

Start with the two rows of card as in the above method. In the next row, pass one shuttle from left to right through the shed, and the other from right to left in the same shed. Leave both ends sticking out ready to be sewn in later. Change the shed and pass the two weft threads through in opposite directions as before. This time do not pull the threads tight, but leave a short loop of weft yarn at each selvedge. Beat this yarn down into place (leaving the loops) and change the shed again.

Pass the two shuttles through once again for the third row. Then take hold of the ends of the weft yarn and by pulling them gently, you will find that the two loops in the previous row are drawn in and you can place the selvedge exactly where you want it.

Continue weaving like this, leaving loops at the end of one row and pulling them in on the next, until you reach the end, when you will have four loose ends to darn in (two at each end). This method may be a little more difficult to master, but once you have done it successfully, you will see that it is much easier to control the selvedges and thus produce a neater, more professional-looking, band.

COLOUR AND PATTERN VARIATIONS

Inkle bands are warp-faced bands, so that in order to achieve patterns with plain weave, it is necessary to thread the colours in different sequences in the warp. The different combinations of colour will give very different weave effects.

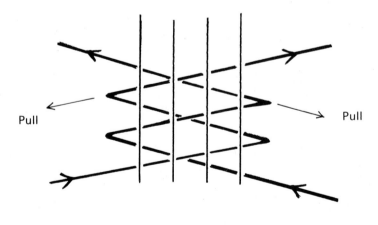

Pull   Pull

Figure 60 Inkle loom weaving — using two shuttles

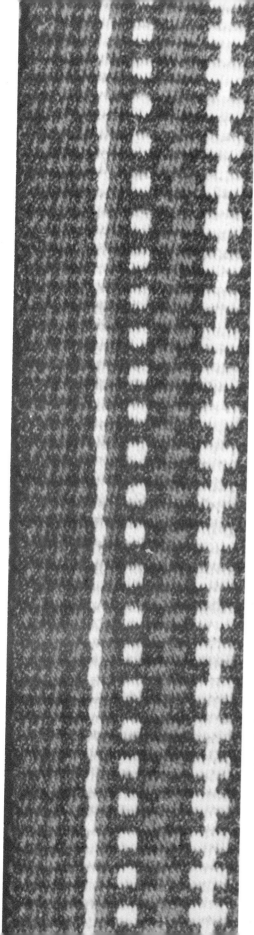

Threading one white thread alternately with one black thread gives stripes of colour across the band. Two white threads, followed by two black threads, give stripes along the length of the band. The more threads of one colour you use together, the wider the stripes you will produce.

A checkerboard effect can be obtained as follows:

a Thread alternate white/black threads, say four threads of each colour (white/black, white/black, white/black, white/black).

b Reverse the sequence and thread black/white alternately, the same number of threads as above.

c Repeat **a** and **b** alternately across the width of the band.

You will find that wherever you change the sequence, there will be two black or two white threads together in the warp. When this warp is woven you will find that you get small blocks of colour instead of stripes. You can of course use any colours, but a bookmark made in black and white checkerboard pattern might make a good present for a chess player!

One variation on stripes which I particularly enjoy doing is a chain effect. Start with at least five threads of the background colour (say white). Then thread two strands of a contrasting colour, followed by one more white, two more of the contrast and then at least five more white to complete the pattern sequence. This design can be used as several repeats over the whole band or one on either edge of the band as a border.

There is of course no need to use one pattern over the whole of the width of the band. A combination of designs and colours can be very effective. One example of a threading is as follows:

Photograph 24 Inkle weaving sampler

```
5 threads colour A
2 threads colour B  ⎫
1 thread colour A   ⎬ chain
2 threads colour B  ⎭
5 threads colour A
1 thread colour C   ⎫ repeat 5 times
1 thread colour D   ⎬ (stripes)
1 thread colour C   ⎭
5 threads colour A
2 threads colour B  ⎫
1 thread colour A   ⎬ chain
2 threads colour B  ⎭
5 threads colour A
```

(Total: 41 threads)

This gives a symmetric design. Asymmetric designs can also work. As an experiment to try out the different widths of stripes, thread up as follows:

1 thread white
1 thread black
2 threads white
2 threads black
3 threads white
3 threads black, etc.

Continue with this sequence, making increasingly wider stripes, until the band is as wide as you want. Keep it as a sampler for later reference.

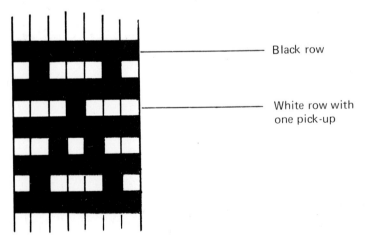

——————————— Black row

——————————— White row with
                one pick-up

Figure 61 Inkle loom weaving – pick-up design

PICK-UP TECHNIQUES

More variation of pattern can be created by using a pick-up stick. Any smooth pointed object will do, and an old knitting needle is very suitable. Thread up the loom for a horizontally striped band (one white, one black alternately) and weave a border of plain weave.

The pick-up technique means that instead of just using the warp threads that are on top of the shed to make the design, some of the underneath threads can also be added to form part of the pattern.

Weave one row with the black threads on top (after weaving a small border). Change the shed and keep the threads apart by inserting your left hand to hold the shed open. With your pick-up stick (or right hand fingers) pick up a few of the black threads from below and leave the pick-up stick in the shed in order to keep these black threads at the top of the shed. When woven, this will produce a white row with a few black stripes in it. Insert the weft thread and change the shed. Weave a plain black row. On the next white row, pick up some more black threads, but do not use the same black warp threads as in the previous pick-up row, or you will end up with large overshot loops of yarn. This technique can be used to weave diagonal stripes or diamonds, and adds interest to the band for a tie or a belt.

IDEAS FOR USING INKLE WOVEN BANDS

The inkle band forms a good firm band if tightly woven, and has many uses. Because it is strong it can be woven in cotton and used as a guitar or camera strap. Belts can be woven in wool or cotton, and finished off with a decorative clasp. If you have woven an article of clothing or want to cheer up a ready-made item, you can make an inkle band to trim the edges. If you have woven the article, you can use the same yarns to make a matching braid. The same applies to bag handles, where the strength of the inkle is needed.

Inkle woven bookmarks make very acceptable presents. Use a fine cotton and set up about fifty threads on the loom. The pattern variations described above can be used very effectively in different combinations to give endless designs. Small pieces of inkle bands left over should not be wasted, and can be attached to key rings, so that you will find it harder to lose your keys!

Men's ties can be woven in about a 4-ply knitting wool. You could use a pick-up design at each end to form a focal point in the design. In the middle section, where the tie goes under the collar, pull the weft yarn in as tightly as you can, to make the band narrower, and less bulky. The pulling in must be done gradually, letting the weft yarn get progressively tighter, and then let it get wider when you weave the last third of the tie.

A novelty idea for Christmas is to weave Christmas tree mobiles. Use either wool or cotton, preferably some yarn that has a metallic thread spun in with it. For the weft you will need about seventeen pieces of cane, ready-cut in lengths, so that the longest one is about 17 cm (7 in), graduating down to the shortest of about 4 cm (1½ in). Set up a warp of about twenty-seven threads, so the braid ends up about 2 cm (¾ in) wide. Leave about 15 cm (6 in) of warp unwoven and then weave 4 cm (1½ in) for the tree trunk. Weave the main part of the tree by inserting one warp thread in one shed and one cane in the next. Start with the longest cane and graduate down to the smallest, inserting them so that only 1 cm (½ in) of the cane sticks out of the left side of the band and the bulk of the canes protrude on the right. The canes are pulled into place to form a triangular shape after the warp is removed from

Photograph 25 Christmas tree mobile

the loom; if the canes are set in place as you weave, you will have difficulty in winding the warp around the loom! After you have finished inserting all the canes, weave another 1 cm (½ in) in plain weave for the top of the tree, pulling in the weft as tightly as possible. You can weave more than one tree on each warp, but remember to leave a gap of at least 30 cm (12 in) unwoven

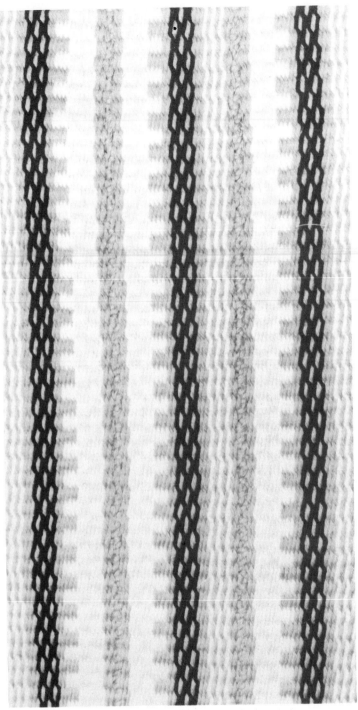

between each mobile. To finish the mobile, knot the ends at the bottom of each tree and tie the top threads on to a ring so that it will hang.

As well as using inkle bands by themselves, they can also be sewn together to make larger articles. Several strips sewn together can be made into a bag, with the strips either going horizontally or vertically.

The round bag shown in the colour plate has three horizontal bands sewn together and nailed on to a circular wooden base to form a bucket bag. The handle is also an inkle band, flat where it joins the sides of the bag, but round on top so that it is more comfortable to hold. In order to weave the round braid, use one shuttle and instead of weaving from side to side, always insert the shuttle from the same side. By pulling the weft hard, the two selvedges will be drawn together and so make the round cord. This technique can also be used to make a very strong cotton dog lead!

You can see that the variations of inkle weaving are endless, and it is a very satisfying form of weaving in its own right. Articles of clothing can be made using strips of inkle bands. A skirt or waistcoat made in this way would be very attractive. Whether you want to weave on a large or small scale, inkle weaving can be adapted to suit your needs and is one of the most interesting forms of weaving.

Photograph 26 Three inkle bands sewn together

8 Backstrap Weaving

The reason for including backstrap weaving at this stage is because it introduces the use of a fixed (or rigid) heddle. There is no loom to make, as the warp is tensioned (as in finger weaving) by the body at one end and a fixed point at the other. However, unlike finger weaving, both warp and weft show in the finished band and the use of the heddle makes the weaving much quicker.

THE RIGID HEDDLE
The rigid heddle is simply a device used both for separating the groups of threads easily to form a shed (gap through which the shuttle can pass) and for beating the weft thread down into place. The heddle is usually made of metal and consists of a solid sheet of metal with holes and slots cut out alternately along its width. When the heddle is used, the warp yarn is thread-

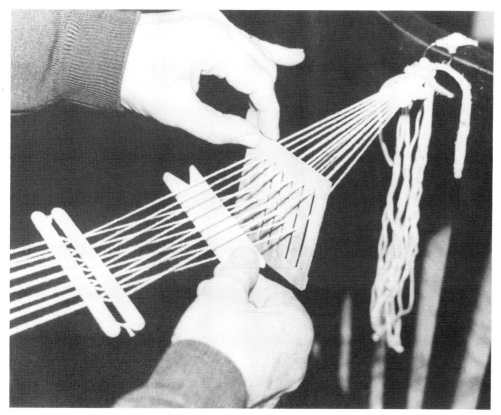

Photograph 27
Backstrap weaving

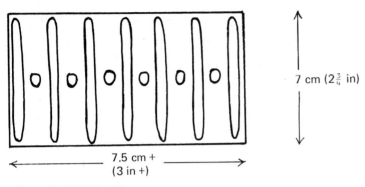

Figure 62 Rigid heddle

7 cm (2¾ in)

7.5 cm +
(3 in +)

The heddle must be strong. The wider it is made, the stronger force is needed in order to raise and lower the heddle, so do not make it very wide at first. The holes and the slots should be as close together as you can reasonably make them without sacrificing too much of the heddle's strength. The depth of the heddle is not critical, so you can make it thicker in order to keep it strong, up to about 1 cm (½ in). The metal ones you can buy have about twelve slots and holes per inch (that is six slots and six holes), so if you can get somewhere near to this, then finer yarns can be used. The thickness of the yarns you can use also depends on the size of the slots and holes, so do not make them too small. Every hole and slot must be very smooth, as if there are any rough edges the warp yarn may catch on them and break. The warp yarn should be able to move easily up and down in the slots.

I have also seen rigid heddles cut out from a thick piece of leather, with a piece of wood nailed top and bottom on the reverse side for support, and these seem to work reasonably well.

ed up so that one thread goes through a slot and the next through a hole, across the whole width of the heddle.

To form a shed using the heddle, it is first lifted up by hand, holding the top of the heddle in the centre. The threads in the holes are thus raised up, whereas the threads in the slots slip downwards, leaving a clear gap between alternate threads. To form the opposite shed, push the rigid heddle down. This time the threads in the holes are pushed down, while the threads in the slots stay on the top. By passing one weft thread through each shed alternately, plain weave is achieved.

This is one piece of equipment that I think it is better to buy. It can be made from wood, but this tends to be rather clumsy, so that the weaver is restricted to using thick yarns. However, you may like to try to make one just to experiment with this technique to begin with, and if so please note the following hints.

SETTING UP THE WARP
Besides the heddle itself, there are one or two other basic items of equipment you will need. In order to thread the warp yarn easily through the heddle, you will need a fine threading hook. These can be bought from specialist suppliers, or made from wire, or a fine crochet hook would do. You will also need one flat stick to tie the warp on to at the front and another for the other end of the warp at the back, plus two lengths of string or braid in order to tie the warp on. Also you will need a stick shuttle on which to wind the weft thread.

First of all cut as many lengths of yarn as you need for the warp, that is one for each hole and slot in the rigid heddle. Knitting wool can be used to start with, bearing in mind the limita-

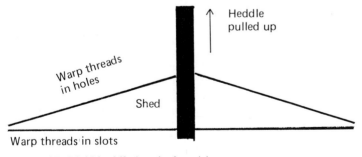

Heddle
pulled up

Warp threads
in holes

Shed

Warp threads in slots

Figure 63 Rigid heddle in raised position

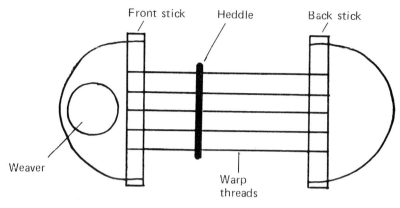

Front stick   Heddle   Back stick

Weaver

Warp threads

Figure 64 Backstrap loom (view from above)

tion in thickness mentioned in the previous section. Cut two extra lengths in order to thread two warp threads double at each edge to make the selvedge stronger. Bear in mind that your finished length of woven material will not be as long as the warp threads, so allow an extra half a metre (yard) to the length which you need to finish up with.

When you have cut all the warp threads you need, begin to tie them one at a time to the back stick, which should be a little longer than the width of the rigid heddle. Tie each thread side by side and space them out as evenly as possible across the whole width. Then secure this stick to a firm object with one long loop of string. Having tied all the warp threads in position, begin from one side and thread each warp in turn through the rigid heddle, taking care that the threads do not cross over each other. Beginning at the left, for example, take the first two threads (selvedge) and, using the hook, pull them through the first slot on the left towards you. Then take the third thread on the stick and pull it through the first hole. Each alternate thread should pass through a hole and a slot, until you end up with the last two threads through the slot on the right hand side of the warp; at this point you will find out if you have done the mathematics correctly!

As you thread the heddle, particu-

larly if it is a wide one, it is just as well to tie a group of threads (say every eight or ten) loosely into a slip knot after they have passed through the heddle. If you do this carefully and you happen to knock the heddle accidentally, you will not lose all your hard work!

The next step is to tie all the warp threads on to the front stick. At this stage, the tension of the warp threads is very important. The threads should be retied on the front stick in their groups of eight or ten. Pass each group over the front stick, then divide the group in half and take them under the stick and over the same warp threads, tying the threads together with the first half of a reef knot (figure 65). This allows the tension to be checked before the threads are finally tied in place. When all the warp threads have been loosely secured, tie the second piece of string on to the front stick and put it around your own waist. With the front and back sticks secured in position, put some tension on the warp by moving your body backwards slightly, but not hard enough to pull the threads off the front stick! Check that the groups of threads are evenly tensioned across the whole width of the warp, as it is all too easy to find that the groups you did last are tighter than the first. The point of leaving the knots loose is so that the threads can easily be adjusted at this stage, until they are even.

67

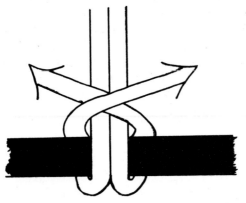

Figure 65 Direction of tension knot used in tying the warp on to the front stick

When this has been checked, the reef knots can be completed.

Next wind the stick shuttle with the weft yarn, and then you are ready to weave. Incidentally, you can use any yarn for the weft, so if you have any oddments of textured yarn, or even some of your own uneven handspun, now is the time to try it out. Remember to insert a stick into the first shed of the weaving, in order to have something hard against which to beat.

WEAVING WITH THE RIGID HEDDLE

To weave with the rigid heddle, first hold it at the top in the centre with one hand and pull the heddle upwards. You will see that all the threads in the holes are pulled up, leaving the threads in the slots to slide to the bottom of the heddle. The gap between the two sets of threads is the shed. Put a stick through the shed and pull it towards you as far forward as it will easily come. This helps to separate the threads in the bunches tied on to the front stick and enables you to start weaving more easily with a firm surface against which to beat.

When you have done this, push the rigid heddle firmly downwards. Now you will find that the threads in the holes are underneath the threads in the slots, so that the position of the threads is the reverse of the first shed. This time, use your stick shuttle wound

with weft yarn and put it through the second shed, leaving a short length of yarn at the beginning (to be woven into the next row). Using the rigid heddle, beat the yarn towards you until it is close up against the stick. For the next row, use the 'up' shed again, putting the beginning of the warp yarn from the first row back into the second row at one side, and thread the second weft row through from the other side. Continue weaving with each alternate shed until the weaving is completed. You will find that you cannot weave the whole length of the warp, since when you near the end there is not enough yarn to be able to lift the heddle up and down to form a shed, but weave as near the end as possible.

It is appropriate to mention tension again at this stage. It is very important in the weft yarn, as well as in the warp. If the weft yarn is drawn across too tightly, the finished piece of weaving will get narrower as you progress. At the other extreme, if it is too loose, there will be loops of yarn left at the selvedges. When you put the weft yarn across, place it at an angle of about 45 degrees to the woven piece, and then beat it into place with the rigid heddle. This is to allow for the take-up in the yarn as it passes over and under the warp threads.

As both the warp and weft yarn show in the finished piece of weaving, obviously the choice of both yarns is very important. The warp yarn must of course be smooth, but you can use more than one colour, either alternate threads of two colours or bands of different colours. For the weft yarn you will need to have one stick shuttle for each individual colour that you use in the weft, so if you decide you want three colours in the weft, make three shuttles. If you use one row of each colour or even just a few rows, there is no need to cut the weft thread off every time, but merely carry the

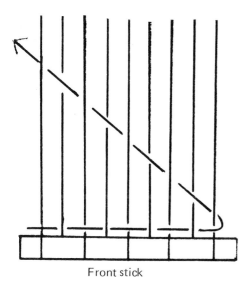

Front stick

Figure 66 Direction of weft thread at 45 degrees to the warp

threads you are not using up the side of the weaving, making sure that the weft threads are caught in at the side at regular intervals to prevent large loops of yarn being left on each selvedge edge! If you want to do wide stripes of weft colour, then weave both ends of the yarn in as you go along, by putting the short end of yarn back into the following shed. The little bits of yarn that still stick out of the weaving after this has been done can be cut off later.

The rigid heddle produces plain weave (over one thread and under the next, etc.). It is important in order to end up with an even piece of fabric, that the rigid heddle is used to beat the weft rows into place as evenly as possible. By this what is meant is make sure that the rows are straight and beaten with the same degree of pressure. If you beat some rows hard and then a few softly, the fabric will look uneven. This is particularly important to watch if you have to stop weaving in the middle of a piece and resume it later. Decide whether you want a tightly woven fabric (for a tweed perhaps) or a softer looser one (for a

scarf) and try to stick to this. To some extent it will depend on the type of yarns you use and you will find out by experimenting how different yarns combined together produce different effects. For your first piece, why not try out a sampler using as many different weft yarns as you can find, both thick and thin, as well as plain and textured — some of the results may surprise you! Colour also can be very deceiving — make a one colour warp and put across it as many different colours as you have; many of the results will not be as you expected.

You will find that after you have woven a few inches, it gets more difficult to lift the heddle as it gets further away from you. At this stage, the woven fabric should be wound on to the front stick, in order to keep the weaving within arm's length. For this you will need one extra shed stick and two pieces of string. Hold the underneath of the front stick and wind it in an anti-clockwise direction so that the woven piece comes over the top stick and rolls on underneath. Leave a short length of weaving still exposed, so that you have something for the rigid heddle to beat against. Then tie the new stick against the front stick on the top to prevent it from unravelling when you start to weave again. Continue weaving and rolling up until you have completed the fabric.

Backstrap weaving is really only suitable for narrow widths of fabric. This is because it gets harder work to lift and push down the heddle, the more threads that are in the warp — a problem which is overcome to some extent on a rigid heddle loom, as described in chapter 11. The advantage of backstrap weaving, like finger weaving, is that it is very portable and ideal for taking away on holiday! The narrow strips can be used for belts, ties, bookmarks, etc., or joined together to form larger pieces of fabric for bags, skirt lengths, for instance.

9 Simple Rigid Heddle Frame

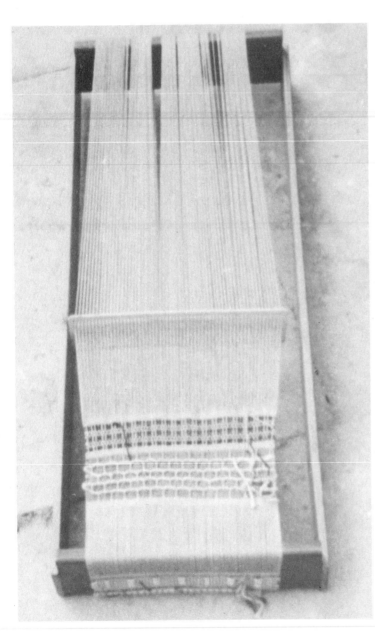

If the idea of backstrap weaving with a rigid heddle does not appeal to you, then perhaps the rigid heddle frame will. Using the frame, you can keep an even tension on the warp threads and it is easier to pick up and put down the work in odd moments when you have a little time to spare. The same rigid heddle can be used as described in the previous chapter, and wider heddles up to about 22 to 25 cm (9 or 10 in) are easier to control using the frame.

MAKING THE FRAME

First get or make your rigid heddle! It is essential that the heddle fits easily inside the sides of the frame, and can be lifted up and down without touching the sides. It is better to make the frame a little too wide than too narrow.

The frame must be strong as there is a lot of tension put on it during weaving. The side pieces can be screwed into position, so that it can be taken apart when not being used, but if storage is no problem then it is better to glue the corners as well. The dimensions given are those to take a standard 22 cm (9 in) rigid heddle, and the side pieces are long enough so that a man's tie or a belt can be woven on the frame. Of course you do not have to weave the full width of the heddle and smaller rigid heddles can be used on the same frame. If you want to weave shorter lengths you will have to make another

Photograph 28 Rigid heddle frame

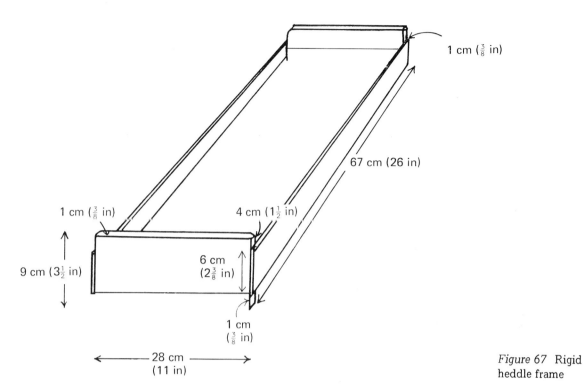

1 cm ($\frac{3}{8}$ in)

67 cm (26 in)

1 cm ($\frac{3}{8}$ in)

4 cm (1$\frac{1}{2}$ in)

9 cm (3$\frac{1}{2}$ in)

6 cm (2$\frac{3}{8}$ in)

1 cm ($\frac{3}{8}$ in)

28 cm (11 in)

Figure 67 Rigid heddle frame

frame with shorter side pieces.

The end pieces are very important. They are set slightly higher at the bottom than the side pieces, so that when the warp is wound around the frame, the threads do not rub on the table. It is also very important that these end pieces are very smooth, and that the top and bottom edges are well rounded. This is because, as the weaving progresses, the warp is pulled around the frame. If the end pieces are not smooth, this will be very difficult to do and any rough pieces may catch and break the warp threads.

USING THE FRAME
In order to thread up the rigid heddle, it has to be held in place in the frame. Cut two pieces of string long enough to tie around the length of the frame. Thread one of these through the hole in the far left of the heddle and tie it

around the frame, end to end. Do the same with the other piece of string, but this time through the hole at the right end. By doing this, the heddle is suspended in position in the frame, leaving both hands free to tie up the warp.

Each warp thread is cut the required length to go right round the frame and be knotted in place. Having measured the right length for this (remembering to allow a bit extra for the knot), cut as many lengths as you need to fill up every hole and slot in the heddle. These can either be all one colour or different colours, but remember that the warp yarn must be strong and smooth, should pass through the holes easily, and should not catch as the heddle is lifted up and down. It is recommended that you start with a thin wool knitting yarn, for making a scarf or table mats.

Each warp thread has to pass either

through a slot or a hole in the heddle (using a threading hook or fine crochet hook), around both ends of the frame and is finally tied in a firm knot on top of the front bar. When you have done this, make sure that the whole thread will slip easily around the frame. If it is difficult, retie it with a looser knot. It is better to have the warp threads too loose than too tight, as they always tend to get tighter as the weaving progresses. If you have some spare warp sticks or pieces of card, they can be taped to the outside of the back bar before you thread up. Then if the weaving gets too tight, simply remove the sticks one at a time as needed during the weaving.

Another word about tension. As with all weaving, it is very important. As you tie each individual warp thread, it is all too easy to get them tighter and tighter as you go along, thus producing an uneven piece of cloth. Try to start threading in the middle of the heddle and work out sideways. It does not hurt if the selvedges are slightly tighter than the centre of the warp, though you should try to guard against this as much as possible.

When you get to threading the edges of the heddle, the two pieces of string can be removed; the centre warp threads will now hold the heddle in position. Thread all the holes and slots in the heddle. Two threads in each of the outer slots help to keep the selvedges stronger.

Rigid heddle weaving always produces plain weave, but there are various ways in which you can produce 'patterns' by using colour changes in the warp and weft. For example, thread up the warp using six black threads and six white threads (or any two contrasting colours) over the whole width of the heddle. When you weave, use the same two yarns in the weft, six rows of black, followed by six rows of white, and repeat this sequence over the whole length of the fabric. The overall effect is of white squares, black squares and grey squares (where black and white are mixed).

Photograph 29 Detail of rigid heddle frame

5 Inkle weave bag, by Evelyn Green

6 Details of a tapestry based on a Van Gogh painting, by the author.

7 Detail of wool scarf in twill weave, by Evelyn Green

8 Detail of cotton place mat in four-shaft pattern weave, by the author

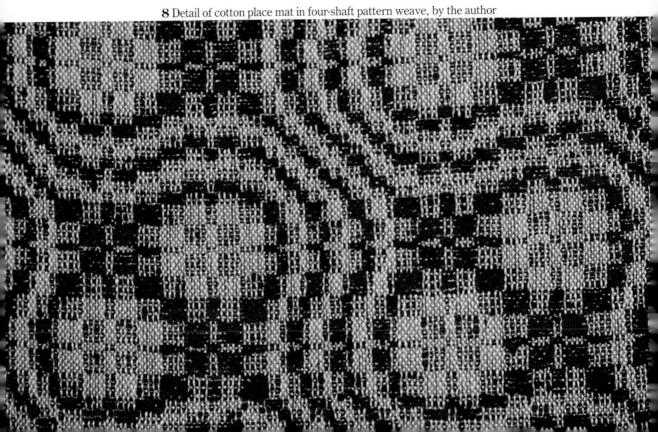

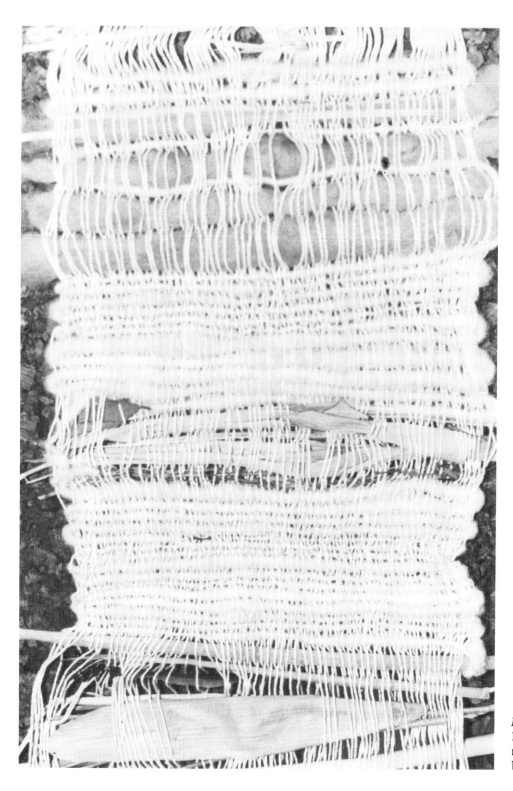

Photograph 30
Hanging woven on a
rigid heddle frame,
by Patricia Allen

73

There are many other alternative colour arrangements that will produce interesting patterns. One white, one black in the warp — two white, two black — two white, one black, etc. One interesting variation on this theme is to thread one black and one white thread alternately for six repeats (twelve threads) and then reverse the sequence threading one white and one black. If you use the same sequence in the weft, a type of log-cabin effect can be woven.

Another way to create patterns is to use a pick-up stick. An ordinary stick is all that is needed, so it can be inserted into the warp behind the heddle. You can use this stick to pick up every fifth thread, for example. Weave the same using the rigid heddle, but every few rows bring the pick-up stick forward near the heddle, thus making a different shed. A thicker weft thread inserted at this point gives a decorative effect, but beware of having loops of yarn which are too long if the article is designed for a practical purpose. Push the stick right to the back of the loom when you are not using it, so that it will not interfere with the two principal sheds.

The pick-up stick can be inserted at any different interval you choose. There is no need to stick to any one particular sequence, but if you want to use more than one stick, it should be inserted in front of the rigid heddle and removed after each row woven.

IDEAS FOR WEAVING
The frame described above is long enough to make a man's straight tie, for which you need only about a 10 cm (4 in) rigid heddle. Fine knitting wool is ideal for this, such as a 2-ply or 3-ply, as it is soft and smooth, and not too bulky to tie. When the tie is woven, weaving as much of the warp as pos-

sible to make it long enough, it can be sewn into a tube, turned inside out and ironed flat so that the seam is down the centre back.

Scarves can also be made on this frame using the 22 cm (9 in) heddle. Use soft knitting wool again for the warp, and a weft of alternate rows of knitting yarn and a soft looped wool yarn can make a very light and attractive scarf. Try not to beat the weft too hard, but just lay it gently into place and straighten it up with the heddle, in order to preserve a light and airy texture. Before you start to weave, think about how you are going to finish off the scarf. If you want a knotted fringe, then remember to leave a good 20 cm (8 in) of warp before you begin by putting in some extra shed sticks. As you can never weave right to the very end of the warp, there should be plenty of spare warp left at the other end to tie the fringe. Tie several threads together with a simple overhand knot, in groups of about four or five threads, and then cut the fringes so that they are even and the same length at both ends.

Table mats are probably better woven in cotton. Leave a gap in the warp between each mat on the frame, by inserting a couple of sticks. It is easier to oversew the ends of the mats while the warp is still under tension on the loom (after removing the sticks) and this should be done to prevent fraying. If you want to make a whole set of matching mats, you will probably be able to make only two or three at a time, because of the limited length of the frame. Make a careful note of the colour sequence of the warp threads, so that you can accurately repeat it for more mats. For a longer length of warp you will need to invest in a rigid heddle loom, as described in chapter 11.

10 Basic Principles of Loom Weaving

Most of the principles of weaving apply to any type of loom where you need to make a long warp to put on it, from the rigid heddle loom and four-shaft table looms described below, to large floor looms and even those with more complicated pattern mechanisms. Basically all looms work on the same principles as the simple looms you can make at home.

Up until now, all that was needed to make a warp was enough lengths of yarn ready cut in order to weave or to wind some yarn around a frame. This is fine for weaving short pieces in fairly thick yarns, but for longer lengths and much finer work, there has to be some way of getting a far greater number of threads on to the loom all at the same tension and without tangling or breaking them in the process. All the looms for which you need to make a warp have some kind of roller device, so that long lengths of cloth can be made — the warp is rolled on at the back and the woven cloth is wound on to a roller at the front.

The directions given in this chapter may sound rather complicated and unnecessary, but do not be put off making or buying a loom. I will try to explain why you need to do each step as we go along, and if you can get a loom and have a try, it should become clearer. It is a case of the task being easy when you know how!

ADVANTAGES OF USING A LONGER WARP

For any readers who are thinking of giving up weaving at this point, let me try and explain why making warps and using bigger looms can be easier once you have mastered the techniques.

The first point is that in the long run it saves time. Instead of setting up and threading the loom for one scarf, you can make one warp and weave four, six or more scarves all on one warp. If you have hundreds of threads in one warp, it can take quite a time to get it all threaded up. Often with very fine warp yarns it may take as much time to set up the loom as to weave the article, so it makes sense to weave more than one article on the same warp.

If you want a matching set of table mats, by having a long warp you can be sure that the warp is identical for all of them, without having to try and repeat the same colour sequence of threads. However, the articles you weave on the same warp need not all be identical. If you use different colours for the weft, you will be surprised at how different each item will be when it is finished — it may even be difficult to tell that they were woven on the same warp!

Using a loom on which you can roll the warp means that you can weave much longer lengths. Fabric for a skirt, dress or coat can be made in one length. Curtains can be woven so that the whole drop is from a single piece of fabric. The possibilities are endless.

MAKING A WARP

A warp consists of a number of threads all the same length. In order to be able to make it, you will need some pegs,

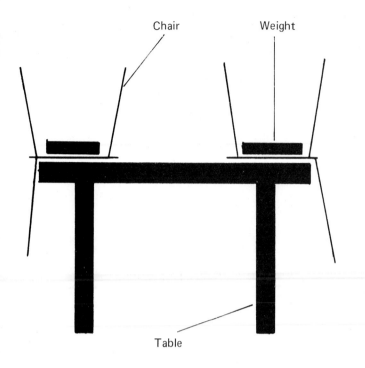

Chair   Weight

Table

Figure 68 Position of chairs on table for making a warp

around which to wind the yarn. The simplest way is to turn two chairs upside-down on a table top and use the upturned legs as the pegs. Put the chairs at either end of a large table. The length of the warp can be up to twice the distance between the two sets of chair legs. If you have a couple of large clamps to clamp the chairs on to the table, this will prevent them from moving during warping, but provided the chairs are fairly heavy and the warp threads are not pulled too tightly, they should not move about too much. Heavy weights put on the chairs (such as a pile of books) will also help.

The chair method is a good way to begin making short warps. However, it is rather limited by the length of the table! To make a longer warp you really need to be able to space more pegs at longer intervals in a zig-zag way, in order to get a long length with the least amount of walking backwards and for-

wards. Some wooden pegs knocked into the lawn (in fine weather!) would do the job, and you can adjust the distance between them in order to make the exact length of warp you need.

A much better way is to make some moveable warping pegs, which can then be clamped on to a table. These can be made with very large nails hammered into small blocks of wood, but a length of wooden broom handle is better, as it is thicker. In any case you will need two sets of double pegs and two or three single pegs to begin with.

A warping frame is better still, as this consists of fixed (or moveable) pegs set in a limited area. It can be hung on the wall to save the chore of walking backwards and forwards along the table. A child's old playpen, cut in half with the spokes smoothed off, makes a good starting point, as the variations in length that can be achieved are enormous. It might be an idea to remove every other peg, as they are set rather closely together.

Having got the equipment ready, plan your warp. What length do you require? Do not underestimate this — allow for fringes, take-up in the weaving of about 7 cm per metre (3 in per yard), plus wastage on the loom of about ½ to ¾ metre (yard), and then allow a bit extra just in case you want to experiment with the weave a little before you begin. It is much better to have too much warp than too little. The extra amount at the end can always be used to make small items such as pin cushions, but the tragedy of having too little warp is that you will have to make and thread up another similar warp just to weave the bit extra to finish the project.

Choose the yarn carefully. Remember it should be smooth and fairly strong. Use just one colour to start with and make a fairly short warp. If you have a cone of wool, put it on the floor and pull the yarn upwards off the top. On the other hand, a spool of

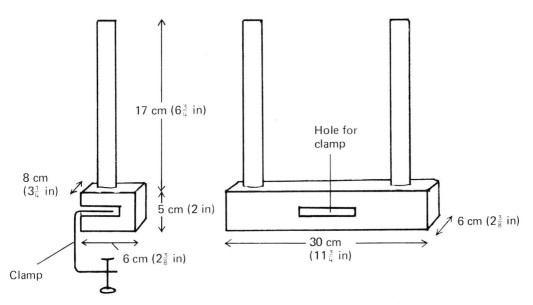

Figure 69 Single and double warping pegs

17 cm ($6\frac{3}{4}$ in)

8 cm ($3\frac{1}{4}$ in)

5 cm (2 in)

6 cm ($2\frac{3}{8}$ in)

Clamp

Hole for clamp

6 cm ($2\frac{3}{8}$ in)

30 cm ($11\frac{3}{4}$ in)

wool should be able to rotate freely; an old shoe box with a knitting needle stuck through the sides allows rotation without the spool travelling all over the floor. More than one spool can of course be put in one box on different needles, provided that the spools do not touch each other. A ball of wool can be put into a waste-paper basket or small cardboard box.

Having worked out the length of your warp, cut a piece of string or contrasting thick yarn to the exact length, plus about an extra 30 cm (12 in). Tie a loop at one end. This string is used to map out the correct path for the warp around the pegs, in order to end up with the right length warp on the loom. You may have to change the position of the pegs several times, before you find the best arrangement.

At this point I should mention that you must have a double peg at each end of the warp for the cross (the reason for this is explained below). If you use chair legs, the path of the warp is shown in figure 72, with alternative paths being represented by dotted lines.

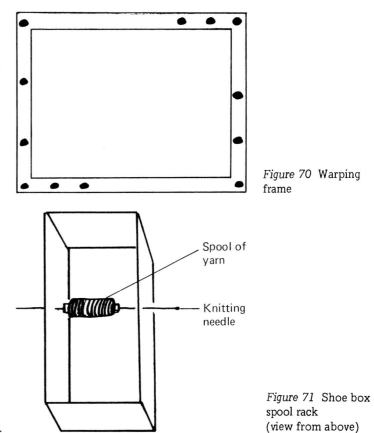

Figure 70 Warping frame

Figure 71 Shoe box spool rack (view from above)

Spool of yarn

Knitting needle

77

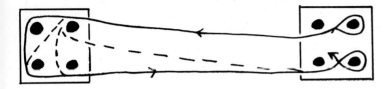

Figure 72 Paths of possible warp threads around chair legs

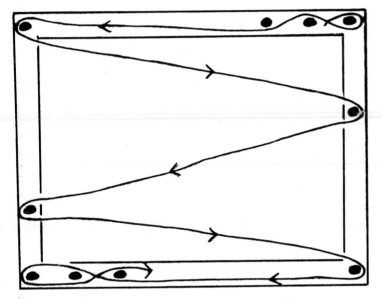

Figure 73 Warping frame showing one possible warp path

The shortest warp possible is of course from chair to chair. Figure 73 shows one of the arrangements possible on a warping frame. Many other combinations are possible depending on the length of warp required. Warping pegs can be clamped in position as required, with a double peg at each end, and as many singles as needed to form a pattern similar to that on the warping frame. Remember that once you have established the way the threads go around the pegs, you must stick rigidly to this path throughout the whole warp, as the threads must all end up the same length to be put on the loom! The point about having double pegs at the beginning and end of the warp is to keep the threads in the correct

order for threading. In a one colour warp, this is not quite so important, but with a sequence of colours, there must be some way of telling which thread comes next when you are threading up the heddles. Also, if the threads are crossed haphazardly they may catch on each other and break. Using the cross, the warp threads are kept in the exact order in which they were wound.

The cross is formed by passing each thread over the previous thread between the two pegs in the opposite diagonal. The thread on each round passes over and under the two pegs, around the end peg, and then back over and under the same two pegs, so that the two sets of threads literally cross over each other in the gap between the two pegs. If you simply remember that the threads should go over and under at each end (O comes before U in the alphabet!), then you will not go wrong.

To start the warp, make a loop at the end of the warp thread and slip it on to the end peg at the top of the frame. Then take it under the second peg and follow the line of the string down to the end of the warp. Remember to make another cross at the bottom and then bring the warp yarn up to the top again, still following the same string line. Make the cross again at the top and continue up and down until you have enough threads for the warp.

Again I have to mention tension. Try to keep the warp threads fairly loose. It is all too easy to let them get tighter and tighter as the warp progresses. Also, as you make the warp, count the threads and tie them in bunches of about ten at a time with an odd scrap of thick contrasting thread — you can do this in a chaining sequence with a long piece of yarn, making another cross after each ten threads. This saves having to count all the threads at once to make sure that

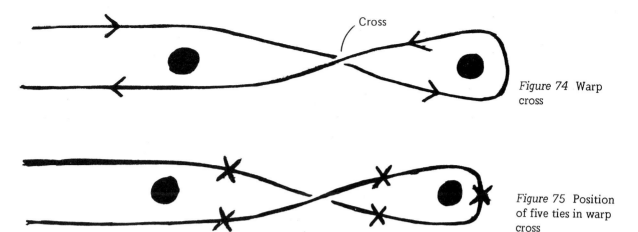

Figure 74 Warp cross

Figure 75 Position of five ties in warp cross

you end up with the right number. Please note that from top to bottom is one warp thread, and when the thread returns again to the top this produces two threads — do the counting at the point where the cross threads intersect at the top.

Before you remove the warp from the pegs, it is vital that the crosses are firmly tied in place. For this you will need some odd scraps of thick yarn in a contrasting colour. Each cross needs *five* ties to keep it secure, as marked in figure 75. Tie these loosely around the warp in the places shown, both for the top and the bottom cross. The counting thread can be removed at this stage.

Only after having carefully checked that the cross is tied securely at both crosses can it be removed from the pegs. Incidentally, one reason why the warp should have two crosses is in case one is accidentally lost at this stage! In order that the warp does not get into a muddle while it is being transferred from pegs to loom, it should be chained. First gently take the bottom cross off the pegs. Hold it in the left hand and with the right, reach through the end loop and pull the next part of the warp loosely through towards you. Holding this new loop in the right hand, reach through it with the left

and pull another loop. Continue this alternately with left and right hands until you reach the top cross. Then take the top cross off the pegs and tie it firmly to the last loop with a thick piece of thread. The warp can then be stored easily until you are ready to use it.

PUTTING THE WARP ON THE LOOM

Having made the warp, now is the time to put it on the loom. For this you will need another piece of equipment: a raddle. The warp somehow needs to be rolled on to the back roller of the loom evenly spaced and roughly the same width as the woven piece will be. Therefore you need a device for quickly spacing the warp across the roller. The raddle in its simplest form is a piece of wood with large nails knocked into it at regular 1 cm (½ in) intervals. It should be made a little wider than the loom itself,

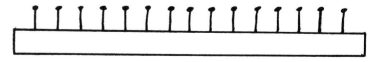

Figure 76 Raddle made with nails

Figure 77 Cross sticks

so that it can be tied on to the side pieces of the loom or clamped on to the top as the warp is being wound on the loom.

You will also need a pair of cross sticks. These are similar to the warp sticks, but have a hole near each end, so they can be tied together in pairs with fine string. Make sure that these are very smooth so that the warp threads do not catch on them. The sticks must be a little wider than the weaving, so that the full width of the warp fits easily between the two holes.

The only other piece of equipment you will need for threading the loom is a threading hook. A fine crochet hook will do for the rigid heddle and even the heddles on a four-shaft loom, but a fine wire hook is better to thread the heddles. This should be made from strong wire and bent to form a small hook at the end. If this is set into a small wooden handle, it is easier to

grip. The best tool for threading the reed is a reed hook, also known as a fish hook because of its shape. This can be made out of thin card, but a fine plastic or metal sheet will wear better. Note that if the edges are too sharp, they may cut the yarn.

In order to put the warp on the loom, it first has to be secured to the back roller. Take the end of the warp that came off the warping pegs last. Find the piece of yarn that kept the threads in order at the end of the warp and took the place of the last warping peg. The threads that were wound around this peg form a loop and, using the tie thread to find this loop, slip it on to the stick attached to the back roller. You will need to untie this stick at one end in order to do this, but tie it back quickly once the loop is in place, so that it is not lost. Check that the place where the stick passes through the warp exactly corresponds with the end tie.

Having done this, fix the raddle to the loom. Where this is done will depend on the individual loom, but it must be fixed firmly, because if it falls off in the middle of winding, all the threads will be lost and you will have to rewind the warp on the loom. If you are using a table loom, try to fix the raddle at the top of the loom above the shafts; in some cases this may not be possible because of the shaft lifting mechanism. When the raddle is firmly clamped or tied in place, get a duster (or any other piece of material), place it over the metal spokes of the raddle and put the chained warp on top of it. This is so that the warp does not sink down in between the spokes of the raddle at this stage. The position of the warp should be that one end of it is attached to the back roller, with the rest of it coming up to the raddle resting on the duster and the other end hanging down over the front end of the loom.

The next step is to put in one cross

Figure 78 Threading hook

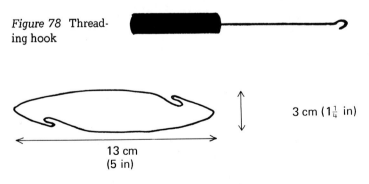

3 cm (1¼ in)

13 cm
(5 in)

Figure 79 Reed hook

80

stick near the back roller, in the space between the two ties furthest away from the back stick. When the cross stick is in place, tie it firmly to the back of the loom, with a piece of string through each hole, so that even if the loom is accidentally moved, the cross cannot be lost when the short warp ties are removed. Check that the warp threads all go around the back stick, the back stick is firmly tied at both ends and the cross stick is secure. Only when you have checked these, can you cut the ties which held the cross in place in the warp.

The next stage is to get the warp spaced evenly over the width of the loom. Having worked out how many threads per cm (in) you need, the threads can now be put into the raddle. Standing at the back of the loom, push the warp and the duster to the far left of the raddle. Take the first group of threads in your right hand (the number of threads you need per cm or in) and place them in the raddle at the right hand edge of the weaving width. If the weaving is for example to be 30 cm (12 in) wide, place the threads in the 15th (12th) space from the centre of the raddle. Use the cross to find out which threads are next in order and handle them carefully, trying not to pull the warp unevenly. Continue to space the warp evenly across the raddle until all the warp threads have been used.

When the raddling has been completed, the loom should be prepared before the warp is wound on to the back roller. This involves securing the cross and the raddle to make sure that even if the loom is accidentally moved (or you have to leave the warp half rolled on), the threads cannot get muddled. The first cross is really finished with at this stage, but just in case the other cross gets lost, insert a piece of string in place of the cross stick, and tie each end of it to the back stick, leaving the string in a loose arc. Only then can the cross stick be removed.

The warp threads are now lying in the raddle. In order to prevent them from jumping out during a careless movement in rolling the warp on, chain the top of the raddle with a piece of string. This involves crossing one thread over another in between each nail, similar to the spacer thread used on a frame loom (see chapter 6). Alternatively you can make a cap for the raddle, which will fit over the nails and, when tied on, will prevent the threads from slipping out of the raddle.

For rolling the warp on the back roller, it is easier if you get someone to help you. One person can turn the back roller, while the other stands at the front of the loom holding the warp under tension. Unchain the warp and make sure that there are no loose threads. If there are any, then gather them up into your hand at the front of the loom, so that there is an even tension over the whole warp. Wind the warp on the roller, a few turns at a time, making sure that none of the threads get caught up in the raddle and break.

At this point you will need some brown paper (newspaper would do provided that the newsprint does not come off and mark the warp!) a little wider than the warp width, but narrow enough to roll on to the back roller.

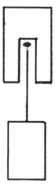

Figure 80 Cap on raddle (side view)

As you wind on, insert the brown paper and let it roll on at the same time as the warp. This separates the layers of warp threads around each turn of the roller. If you have any spare shed sticks you can use these instead, inserting them at regular intervals. The reason for this is to stop the warp threads from sinking down into previous warp layers and producing an uneven tension.

Great care should be taken at all times to keep an even tension on the warp. The more carefully you prepare the loom, the easier you will find it to weave. Carry on rolling until most of the warp is on the back roller. Leave enough in front so there is plenty to thread through the heddles and tie on to the front stick. Remove the raddle by taking off the cap or the chaining, and lift the warp carefully out of the slots.

Before you actually begin to thread the loom, the front cross must be transferred from the end of the warp, to near the back of the loom, and the cross sticks inserted. Find the two warp ties holding the cross furthest away from you and gently begin to pull the threads apart. A smooth yarn may pull apart very easily, but if the yarn is at all sticky, then you may need to do it thread by thread until the gap between the two sets of threads reaches the back bar. Insert the first cross stick in this gap and tie it firmly to the back bar, so that there is no danger of losing the cross if the loom is accidentally knocked or moved. Once you are sure that this side of the cross is safely tied at the back of the loom, the two ties holding it in the warp can be cut away.

In transferring the second part of the cross to the back, pull apart the next two ties on the warp. You may find this side a little harder to move, but be patient and if necessary do it thread by thread, in order to avoid breaking any warp yarn. When this cross is at the back of the loom, insert the second cross stick and, with a piece of string through each hole, tie it loosely to the first cross stick, leaving a gap of about 2.5 cm (1 in) between the two sticks. The two ties on the warp holding this side of the cross can then be cut away, leaving just one remaining tie in the end of the warp.

THREADING

Unless you deliberately intend to thread the heddles with double threads, the end of the warp has to be cut. Using the last tie as a guide, cut through the loop at the end of the warp.

At this stage it is a good idea to divide the warp in half and start threading from the middle of the heddles. On some looms you may have to do this because of the way the shafts are tied in the middle, as it is difficult to move heddles from one side to the other without untying the shafts.

Details of how to thread a rigid heddle loom and a four-shaft loom are given in the appropriate chapters. However, securing the groups of threads once they are threaded and tying on to the front roller is common to both.

After you have threaded about eight or ten threads through the heddle or reed, tie them together loosely to avoid the danger of having to rethread if they are accidentally pulled out of the heddle or reed. Also if you are threading a four-shaft loom for a pattern weave, it helps to keep a count of the threading sequence.

For tying on to the front stick, use the same knot as described for back-strap weaving. Again work from the centre outwards and be careful to keep an even tension on the warp threads.

WEAVING ON A LOOM

One of the advantages of a loom compared to a frame is that you can adjust the overall tension. Keep it fairly tight when weaving, but slacken it when the loom is not being used. The tension you keep when weaving depends on personal preference. It should be taut enough so that the weft can be beaten down easily, yet not so tight that it is hard work to raise and lower the heddle or shafts.

It is only when you begin to weave that you will find out how well the warp was made! An uneven warp may mean that loose threads fall into the shed and are caught and broken as the shuttle is passed across.

Broken warp threads should be mended as soon as they are discovered. The easiest way if the yarn is fairly thin is to join the two broken ends by knotting in a piece of yarn of a good contrasting colour, continue to weave as before, and then darn in the missing thread when the weaving has been taken off the loom. The darning thread must be the same as the broken warp thread and the ends should be well overlapped to prevent a hole from appearing later on.

It is not possible to use this method if the knot sticks in the heddle or reed. Then a substitute warp thread has to be added, using the same yarn as the broken thread. You will need to have a long length of spare warp yarn in order to do this. The broken warp thread coming from the back of the loom should be taken back to near the back roller. Tie the substitute thread to it in a bow (this will need to be undone and retied several times). The substitute warp thread should then be rethreaded in heddles and reed, and brought to the front of the loom. Insert a pin in the woven fabric across the width of the fabric, at the point where the thread is broken, and wrap the substitute warp thread around it at the correct tension. Weave on as before. When the warp is rolled on and the bow at the back comes nearer the heddles, undo it and retie the bow near

the back roller again. Continue this sequence until the original broken warp thread is long enough to reach the woven fabric at the front. At this point it should be brought back into the weaving by inserting another pin as above. The substitute warp thread should then be ignored.

When the finished cloth is taken off the loom, both ends of the broken thread must be darned into the fabric so that they overlap. The above procedure also applies if you find a knot in the warp yarn.

A word here about the cross sticks. There are two schools of thought about their use during the weaving process: one says that they must be left in and the other says that they must be taken out! I prefer to leave them in, because it prevents any warp threads crossing and getting caught up in the heddles. It also helps maintain tension, though care must be taken when rolling on the warp, to make sure warp threads are not broken by being caught up in the sticks. The only reason I can see for taking them out is if they hinder the formation of the shed. Some looms do not have much space at the back between the shafts and the back bar. In this case, removing the cross sticks while weaving means that it is possible to get a better shed.

The formation of the shed also determines when to roll the warp on the loom. The amount of weaving you can do before rolling on each time depends on the individual loom. When the weaving gets very near the heddle or reed, you will find it more difficult to get the shuttle through the shed. The chances of getting the end of the shuttle caught in a warp thread and breaking it are greater at this point. When rolling on, first loosen the back roller and then wind on from the front. Do not use too much force for this, but if it is stiff, check to see that there are no warp threads caught in the cross sticks or heddles.

CALCULATIONS

Up until now you have just used a suitable warp thread for whatever you want to make. However, when you make a warp, the calculations need to be a little more precise, as you must make sure you have enough yarn to finish the project.

One quick way to estimate roughly is to take a ready-made article similar to what you want to make and weigh it. For example, a set of table mats in fine cotton may weigh approximately 170 g (6 oz). Assuming that the warp and the weft are of the same yarn, it would take approximately 85 g (3 oz) for each. Warp wastage must be added to this, both for tying on the loom and for the space between each mat, so allow roughly an extra 85 g (3 oz). This means that you would need about 255 g (9 oz) of the fine cotton. If you are buying the yarn, then buy about 350 g (12 oz) — it is always useful to have some bits of yarn left over with which you can experiment, but a disaster if you run out of yarn before the end and cannot get any more! Always try to overestimate your requirements, and if possible build up a small stock of yarns, even small bits, so that you can try out new ideas and mixtures of colour.

If you are handspinning the yarn, make sure you have enough fleece. From the raw fleece, you will obtain about half to three-quarters of the fleece weight of yarn. This is because there is usually some dirt in the fleece when you get it, and there is more weight loss when the grease is removed during washing. So from a fleece weighing one kilo, you would get about 500 g (1 lb) to 750 g (1½ lb) of spun yarn.

The yarn count system is a more precise way of telling what length you can expect in a particular weight of yarn, though until you get used to the numbers it can seem rather daunting. Cotton for example has 840 yards to the lb if the count is 1. If you see a 6s yarn, it will have 6 x 840 yards to the lb and will therefore be a much finer yarn than a 1s. A 2/6s cotton is two strands of 6s cotton plied together, and will therefore have half as many yards per pound as the 6s cotton. Incidentally it is always better to use a plied yarn for warp, as it is usually stronger and will not tend to stick. A 2/6s cotton is a good medium weight cotton for table mats and will thread easily through a manufactured rigid heddle.

Wool is more complicated, as there are several different count systems depending on where it was spun. The most common is the Yorkshire Skein Woollen, which has 256 yards per 450 g (1 lb). So a 15 cut wool ('cut' is the name for the woollen count) would contain 256 x 15 yards per 450 g (1 lb).

If you are using knitting yarns, then the approximate lengths per 50 g (1¾ oz) ball are as follows:

3-ply – 280 metres (300 yards)
4-ply – 175 metres (190 yards)
Double knitting – 115 metres (125 yards)
Triple knitting – 70 metres (75 yards)

You can see from these figures that the thicker the yarn, the less length you get per ball. The above figures, however, should serve only as a rough guide, and may vary a bit depending on the yarn content and the manufacturer. Please also note that just because a knitting wool is called '4-ply', it does not necessarily have four strands of yarn plied together. The term '4-ply' is specifically one used in the knitting wool trade to denote a certain thickness of yarn.

If you have some yarn but do not know the count, as for example your handspun wool, the only way to estimate it is to compare it with some yarn of which you do know the count. If you want to knit your handspun wool, the only way to find a suitable pattern is to compare it with a manufactured knitting yarn and then use the knitting pattern for that yarn, being careful to do a tension square first, just to check.

In order to find out how much yarn you will need to make a warp, first find out the correct yardage per 450 g (1 lb) or estimate as nearly as possible if the exact count is not known. You will also need to work out how long a warp you want and how many ends per cm (in) you will need. On a rigid heddle this is fixed by the number of holes and slots in the heddle, and details for four-shaft looms are given in chapter 13. If you then multiply the number of threads (ends) in the warp by the length of each warp thread, you will be able to find the number of metres (yards) needed to make the warp. Divide this by the metres (yards)

per 450 g (1 lb) and you will know how much yarn you need to buy. This can be set out as follows:

$$\frac{\text{number of ends x length of warp}}{\text{yards (metres) per 1 lb (450 g)}}$$

Having done these calculations, you can then make the warp, knowing that you will have plenty of yarn to finish the project. This is particularly important if you are buying yarn, as the supplier may not be able to repeat the same dye lot at a later date. You can often buy ends of lines or odd dye lots of yarn quite cheaply, but of course they will not be repeatable.

All the above methods and calculations apply to most types of hand loom. There are of course variations in the methods of threading and these are described in the relevant chapters.

11 Using a Rigid Heddle Loom

The rigid heddle loom has two basic advantages over the rigid heddle frame. Firstly you can put on a long warp and make lengths of material for skirts, jackets, etc. Secondly you can weave wider widths of cloth, because the supports at the side of the loom hold the rigid heddle in place while you are weaving, thus leaving both hands free to throw the shuttle.

MAKING THE LOOM
Figures 81 and 82 show the main pieces of the loom. The front and back pieces both need to have a roller bar near the base, but not touching the table. This is particularly important on the front roller, as the finished cloth is wound around this and there must be enough clearance so that the material does not rub on the table.

The rigid heddle is fitted into a wooden bar, so that it can rest in the slots on the side supports and be lifted up and down easily. This makes the weaving easier, as you will be able to take your time in passing the shuttle through the shed and placing it in the right position before beating down into place. The drawings for the loom will take a 40 cm (15 in) rigid heddle, though you can use a wider one if you want, but the dimensions would have to be increased in order to accommodate the extra width. In any case there must be plenty of space between the side pieces, so that the heddle can move up and down freely without touching the sides.

The rollers should be made so that

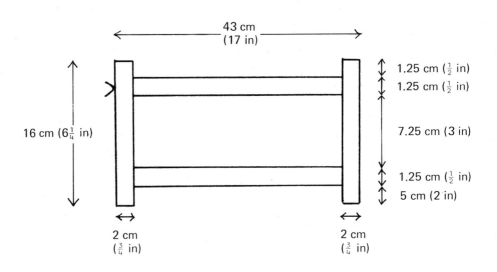

Figure 81 Rigid heddle loom (front and back bars)

43 cm (17 in)

16 cm ($6\frac{1}{4}$ in)

1.25 cm ($\frac{1}{2}$ in)
1.25 cm ($\frac{1}{2}$ in)
7.25 cm (3 in)
1.25 cm ($\frac{1}{2}$ in)
5 cm (2 in)

2 cm ($\frac{3}{4}$ in)

2 cm ($\frac{3}{4}$ in)

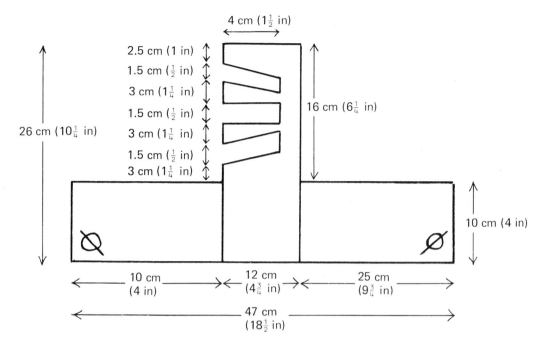

Figure 82 Rigid heddle loom (sides)

they can be rotated and then held in several different positions — by this method the warp tension can be adjusted and kept even. A ratchet is the best way of doing this (fitted outside the side pieces), but as it is sometimes difficult to obtain, a wooden peg system will work adequately. One of these should be made for the back roller and one for the front, both to be fitted to the right hand side of the loom.

Once again, the wood used must be strong and all surfaces should be smooth. You will also need to make several stick shuttles (one for each weft colour you intend to use), a pair of cross sticks and at least two shed sticks (flat pieces of wood slightly wider than the weaving width) to attach to the back and front rollers.

When you have made the loom, drill three holes, evenly spaced through the back and front rollers. Cut a length of

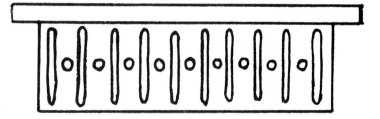

Figure 83 Rigid heddle mounted in bar

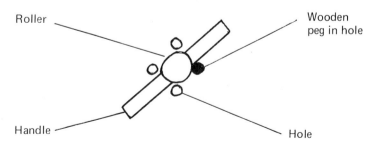

Figure 84 Tension handle on front and back rollers

87

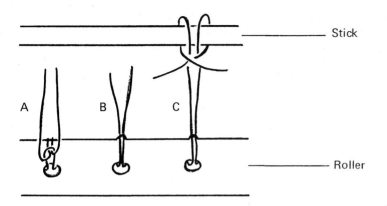

Figure 85 Tying sticks on to the loom (back and front)

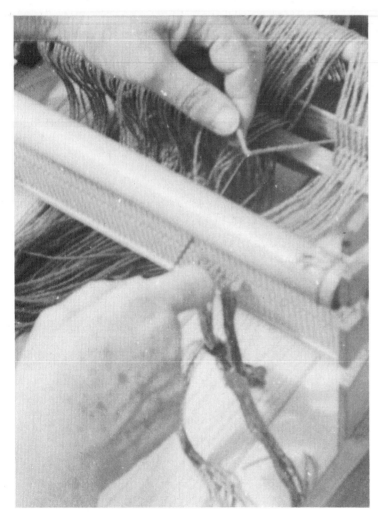

strong string about 1 metre (1 yard) long, fold it in half to find the midpoint and insert this loop through one of the holes. Thread the two ends through this loop after it has passed through the roller and pull tight. Do this for all the holes in the back and front rollers. The shed sticks should then be tied on to these strings, one each on the back and front rollers. For this, use the adjustable tension knot as described for backstrap weaving, making sure that the sticks are tied parallel to the rollers.

WEAVING ON THE RIGID HEDDLE LOOM

Make a warp as described in the previous chapter, and roll it on to the back roller of the loom. Using a threading hook or a fine crochet hook, thread the heddle, starting at one end and passing each thread in turn through a hole and a slot. If the warp is not to be as wide as the heddle, you will have to start a little way in from the side, making sure that the warp ends up centrally placed on the loom. Loosely tie the warp threads in groups in front of the heddle, so that they do not slip back.

In order to thread the warp in the correct order, use the cross sticks, which have been transferred near to the back roller. As each alternate thread goes under and over each stick, it should be obvious which thread comes next in the sequence. When threading, it is a good idea to tie the heddle into the middle slot of the side supports to prevent it from being accidentally knocked out of place. A couple of rubber bands are useful for doing it quickly.

Having threaded the loom, tie the threads in groups on to the front stick, using the adjustable tension knot. Start

Photograph 31 Threading the rigid heddle

88

from the centre group and work out to each side, checking the tension to get it as even as possible. When you have tied all the small groups of warp threads, make sure the tension is even across the whole warp and then knot the threads firmly to secure them in place.

Before you begin to weave, a shed stick should be inserted in the first shed. Having inserted it, form the opposite shed and check that the heddle is correctly threaded, and that there are no gaps in the heddle or any crossed threads. It is much easier to correct mistakes at this stage. Check also that there is enough distance at the back between the rigid heddle and the cross sticks, so that there is a good shed between the threads when the heddle is lifted or depressed. If the shed is not very good, slacken the warp and carefully move the cross sticks around to the back of the loom, just above the back roller.

The two sheds for plain weave are obtained alternately by lifting up and pushing down the heddle. In order to keep the heddle in place, leaving both hands free to manipulate the shuttle, push the ends of the heddle bar into the side supports of the loom. The tension is very important in order to obtain a good shed: too tight and it will be hard work to lift — too loose and the shed will not be clear. If an even shed is difficult to form, check the tension, as one or two loose threads may hang down into the space. If the warp yarn used is too hairy, the threads may tend to stick to one another. In this case you may have to coax the threads gently into their places with each row. This slows down the weaving process considerably and can cause broken warp threads. Learn from your mistakes, however, and do not use the same yarn again for warp!

In order to help clear the shed, pull the heddle up from the middle position on the loom, draw it towards you (still in the raised position) and then place it in the upper slot. Repeat this process, holding the heddle down in the opposite shed. The sequence of weaving on the rigid heddle is as follows:

1 Take the heddle out of the side pieces, pull it upwards and towards you, and then replace it in the upper slot.
2 Pass the shuttle across in between the two sets of threads, leaving the weft thread at an angle of about 45 degrees.
3 Beat the weft thread into place using the heddle.
4 Push the heddle down, draw it towards you and then insert it into the bottom slot.
5 Pass the shuttle through the weaving in the opposite direction, again leaving the weft thread at a 45 degree angle.
6 Beat the weft thread into place using the heddle.
7 Repeat this whole sequence, until sufficient length is woven to complete the project.

Having done this sequence several times, you will find that you soon develop a rhythm of weaving. It is important that the weft is beaten evenly into place, as heavy and light beating will show up in the finished cloth. Also try to keep the selvedges even, by not pulling the weft in too tightly or leaving loops at the side. Weave slowly to start with, checking carefully as you go along, and with practice you will find that these things are done automatically.

When you find that it is getting more difficult to obtain a good shed, you will have to wind on the warp. To do this, first undo the back roller to slacken off the warp and replace the peg one or two holes further on. Then undo the front roller and tighten the warp by rolling the already woven cloth around the front roller. Replace the peg in the front roller to achieve a good weaving tension and continue weaving again.

Carry on weaving and rolling on until you have woven as much of the warp as possible. Then cut the warp off the back stick and pull the warp ends back through the heddle. Unwind the finished weaving from the front roller and untie or cut the warp threads from the front stick. It is just as well to finish off the ends of the weaving as soon as possible to prevent fraying. Either knot the warp threads together in small groups, or hemstitch, oversew or machine the ends neatly. If you have used handspun wool or a wool weaving yarn which is still in the grease, the finished cloth should be handwashed in soapflakes and this will help the fibres to knit together and stop the fabric fraying so much when it is cut.

If you plan to weave a set of matching table mats on the same warp, measure them carefully as you go along, so that they all turn out roughly the same length. Remember to weave them slightly longer than you need, as if they are measured under tension, the mats will not be quite as long as you think when they are taken off the loom. If the mats are to match exactly, keep a careful note of the weft colour sequence used in the first mat and the width of the stripes, so that you will be able to repeat them exactly for the rest of the set — the first one will of course 'disappear' around the front roller as it is woven!

It is also important to leave enough spare warp between the mats if you intend to knot the fringes, and this should be allowed for in your calculations. Insert a stick in the warp before you begin to weave each mat, as this gives something hard against which to beat and helps to keep the first few rows straight. Another idea is to oversew the ends of the mats, and some people find it easier to do this while the warp is still under tension on the loom.

Although you are restricted to plain weave on the rigid heddle loom, many 'patterns' can be obtained using colour changes in warp and weft. For example, if you warp the loom using six dark threads alternately with six light threads, and then use the same yarn for weft, six rows of each colour, this gives a check pattern. One interesting weave is to thread one light thread and one dark thread alternately five times and then repeat this sequence using one dark thread followed by one light thread five times. When woven with the same colour sequence, it gives a log cabin effect. There are of course hundreds of different patterns to be obtained using colour changes, so you can experiment and see the effects these have. Try also different weft sequences on the same warp, and this way obtain different patterns on the same threading. When you find a pattern you like, it is just as well to keep a note of how you wove it, in case you want to repeat it for another project.

IDEAS FOR WEAVING

The following are just a few ideas to get you started, as once you have woven a few things, you will be able to think of lots more yourself.

Scarves are useful items to weave and make good presents. Use a soft wool warp — a fine knitting yarn or Shetland wool are both very good. Looped wool yarns can be used for the weft, which should be beaten very lightly in order to produce a soft open fabric. To make it even lighter, try using a spaced warp. This means that instead of threading every hole and slot in the heddle, you leave one or two empty to give a gap in the warp; you will have to take this into account when you calculate the number of warp threads to make. When you do this, remember that the sequence of one thread through a hole followed by one thread through a slot must still be continued. So if you decide to miss some threads, these must be an even number (say two holes and two slots) so that the last thread on one side is through a hole and the first thread on the other is in a slot. This technique produces a much more open fabric and the looped wool weft helps to keep the threads apart. Knot the warp threads in groups at each end, wash gently by hand in soapflakes, and then finish off by cutting the fringes evenly at each end.

Table mats can be woven in cotton, or using a cotton warp and wool (handspun) weft. Incidentally, a word about mixing different fibres. It is fine to have a warp of one yarn (cotton) and a weft of another (wool), but beware of mixing fibres in either warp or weft. If you weave stripes of say, wool and cotton and linen, you will have problems when the article is washed because of the different rates of shrinkage, and may end up with something totally unusable. So stick to one fibre one way and you should be all right. (Mixing fibres is acceptable in wall hangings, as these are not liable to be washed.)

Other uses for handspun and dyed wool on the rigid heddle are cushion covers, bags, waistcoats, skirts and table mats. Unless your handspun wool is very evenly spun, it is not recommended for warp. Use a machine-

spun wool or cotton, depending on the end product you want.

It is possible to weave clothing fabrics, even on a narrow rigid heddle loom. To weave enough for a skirt, you will have to calculate the length of skirt required, and then weave enough cloth to enable it to be made up in four or five panels, depending on the width of the heddle and the style of the skirt. Some weavers are nervous about cutting up materials they have woven. If the woollen fabric is fully shrunk after it has been woven, then it should not fray so easily.

In order to do this, the fabric must be 'milled' after it has been removed from the loom. Immerse the fabric in hand-hot water with enough soapflakes to make a good lather. Pound the material up and down for at least five to ten minutes, until you can see that the fibres in the material have started to felt together. Thoroughly rinse the material, and while it is still damp, roll it on to a wooden or thick cardboard roller (if cardboard, it will have to be covered with a thin plastic sheet first). Use a thin sheet of material wound around the roller with which to secure the first end of fabric, securing the last end with a nail bar (thin bar of wood with nails hammered through it — the points of the nails stick into the material and hold it firm). The nail bar is held in position

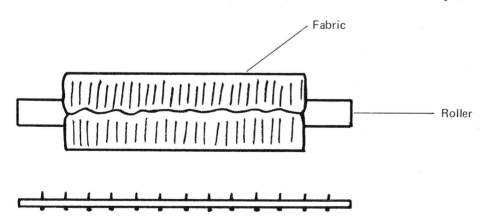

Figure 86 Drying roller with fabric rolled on

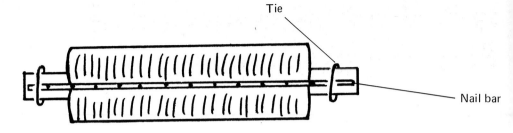

Tie

Nail bar

Figure 87 Drying roller with end of fabric secured with nail bar

with string ties at both ends. The material should be rolled around the roller as tightly as possible, making sure that any stripes in the fabric are straight — if they are put on crooked they will dry that way! Leave the material to dry naturally over several days. When the outside is dry, take off the material and re-roll it the other way around, so that the wet material that was inside gets a chance to dry. When the material finally comes off the roller, it should be ready for use, and will probably not even need ironing. If this milling is not done then the material may shrink after washing.

Another idea for the rigid heddle loom is to use it in combination with the tapestry techniques as described in the chapter on frame loom weaving. This time the heddle is used only as a means of separating the warp threads and the weft is beaten down as hard as possible with a fork or tapestry beater. Using the heddle in this way speeds up the weaving process, and the rollers on the loom mean that you can weave a longer length than on a frame.

12 A Short Introduction to Four-Shaft Weaving

It is beyond the scope of this book to give plans for making a four-shaft table loom. However, there are some detailed plans available in some of the recommended books, and if you are keen to progress with your weaving, this is the next stage to think about. Having four shafts enables you to do more complicated weaving patterns and use a much greater variety of yarns. The purpose of this chapter is simply to give you some idea of what you can achieve with a more complicated loom.

There are on the market some two-shaft table looms, which might be regarded as a stepping stone between the rigid heddle loom and the four-shaft loom. In my opinion, it is not worthwhile taking the trouble to build such a loom. The only advantages of this over the rigid heddle loom are that you can use a greater variety of yarns in the warp (from thick to thin) and you may be able to weave a greater width. Most people find that when they want to progress, it is the possibility of weaving more complicated patterns that intrigues them, and the four-shaft loom opens up a tremendous variety of patterns.

HEDDLES, SHAFTS AND REEDS

Using a four-shaft table loom is not much more difficult than using a rigid heddle loom, but the possibilities are even more fascinating. The warp is put on in exactly the same way as for the rigid heddle loom, using the raddle. It is in the threading up that more care is needed.

There is, however, one more calculation that you need to make before you can make a warp for this type of loom — how many threads per cm (in) do you need? On a rigid heddle loom, this is governed by the number of holes and slots in the heddle, but on a four-shaft loom you can use as few or as many of the moveable heddles as you like. The number will depend on the width you want to weave and the thickness of the warp yarn.

To find out how many threads per cm (in), use a ruler and wind the warp thread around it so that each thread just touches the one next to it. Wind about 1 cm (½ in) and count how many times the yarn goes around the ruler. This is the number of threads you will need to use per 2 cm (1 in) if the weft is to be about the same thickness of yarn and you intend to do plain weave. If you want to use a different weft yarn or do a pattern weave, this figure may have to be altered, but it is useful as a rough general guide.

If you know the weft yarn you are going to use, then you can wind one thread of this and one thread of the warp yarn around the ruler, laying each thread side by side. This time wind about 2.5 cm (1 in) and count the number of *warp* threads in that distance; this will give you the number of threads per cm (in). If you want to do tapestry weaving where it is only the weft that will show in the finished piece, you will need to set the warp at a lesser number of threads per cm (in) in order to make sure that the warp is completely covered. For the warp-faced fabric, the opposite is true.

Having worked out how many threads per cm (in), multiply this by the width of the fabric you want and this will give you the total number of threads needed for the warp (plus two extra for the selvedge). Work out the length of the warp you need, bearing in mind that you will have at least ½ metre (½ yard) of wastage that cannot be woven. Make the warp and put it on the loom. The raddle should be fixed on top of the bar above the shafts (the highest part of the loom), but this may not be possible because of the heddle lifting mechanism. In this case, fix it on to the sides at the back of the loom, parting the heddles in the middle and removing the reed; the warp should then be rolled on through the gap in the middle of the shafts, taking care that the warp threads do not come out of the raddle. When the warp is rolled on and the cross transferred to the back, you are ready to start threading.

The heddles on a loom are made either from string or metal and the supports which hold them in place are called the shafts. A heddle (or heald) is simply a single piece of string or wire, tied or bent into three loops. The eye of the heddle is the small loop in the centre through which each

warp thread is passed, one thread per heddle. This is so that when the shafts are raised, the threads in the heddles on the one particular shaft will also be raised to form the shed. More than one shaft can be raised at any one time, the sequence depending on the pattern. The shafts consist either of a metal frame (usually with metal heddles) or two wooden bars, one top and one bottom (for use with string heddles). The lifting mechanism varies on different table looms, but usually it is by means of levers, either at the side or on the top, one lever to each shaft.

The way a pattern can be woven depends on two things: the order in which the heddles are threaded and the sequence in which the shafts are lifted. For plain weave, the heddles are threaded 1, 2, 3, 4 (taking shaft one to be the shaft at the front of the loom nearest the weaver), and this sequence is repeated over the whole width of the warp. Check the threading carefully as you go along and tie the threads loosely in front of the heddles in groups as they have been checked. To thread the heddles you need a threading hook, though some weavers find it easier to thread string heddles just using their fingers.

If the shafts are lifted by a central string, the only way to transfer heddles from one side to another across the width of the shafts is to untie this string. The way to avoid having to do it too often is to divide the warp in half and start threading from the centre out to one edge, then back to the centre and out to the other edge. Also do make sure that you have enough heddles on each shaft before you begin threading. More string heddles can easily be made on a board of wood with four nails knocked into it. Use a thin strong string that will not stretch or slip. Beginning at the top, loop the string around the top nail, tie it tightly around the second,

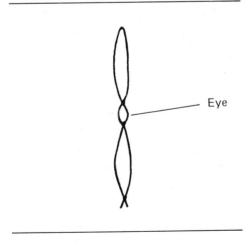

— Eye

Figure 88 String heddle

94

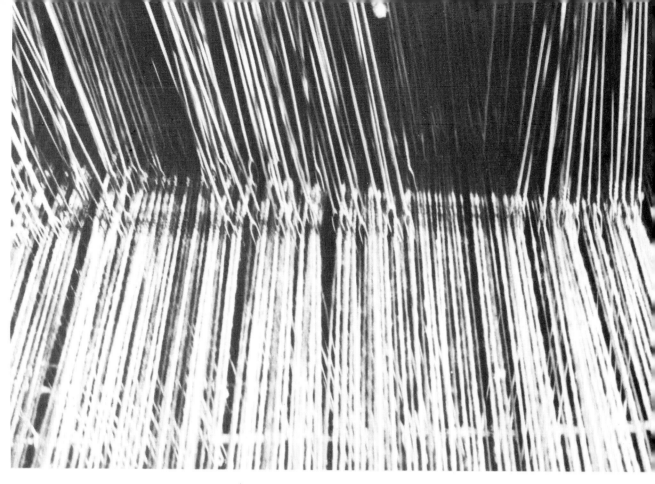

Photograph 32 Warp threads passing through the eyes of the heddles

then again around the third to make the eye, and finish off by tying it around the bottom nail. It takes time if you want to make all your heddles in this way, but it is useful if you need to make a few extra for a special project.

The heddles are threaded according to a predetermined sequence. The most simple of these is 1, 2, 3, 4, and repeat this over the whole width of the warp. In order to obtain plain weave, every alternate thread must be raised. So if you lift shafts 1 and 3 together to form one shed, and then shafts 2 and 4 together for the opposite shed, this will give plain weave. There are many other sequences of threading and lifting.

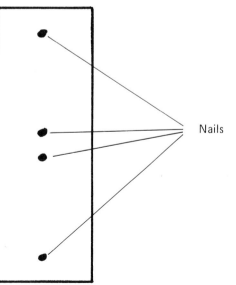

Nails

Figure 89 Board for making string heddles

95

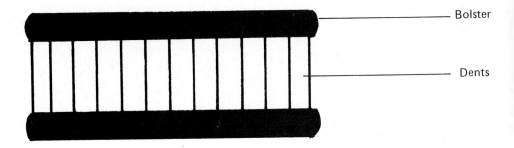

Figure 90 Reed

When the heddles have been threaded, the warp yarn should be passed through the reed. This is like a large metal comb, but closed on both sides. The spaces in between the 'teeth' are known as dents, and the number of dents varies from reed to reed. One of the most common is 40/10 (40 dents per 10 cm or approximately 10 dents per in). The reed has two functions: firstly to space the warp threads evenly and secondly to beat the weft threads into place. The size of the reed you will need varies from project to project. For a thick warp thread for weaving a rug you will need about a 20/10 (approximately five dents per in) reed. Very fine yarns require anything up to about a 100/10 (approximately 25 dents per in), but handweavers generally would not use yarns as fine as this.

However, if you do decide to make a table loom, there is no need to buy a vast selection of reeds. One large reed, say a 20/10 (approximately five dents per in) and a 55/10 (approximately 12.5 dents per in) are all you need to start with. The reeds can be threaded in many different combinations to obtain different setts (number of threads per cm or in). For example, a 55/10 (approximately 12.5 dents per in) reed can be threaded with two threads in each dent, giving 110 threads in 10 cm (approximately 25 threads per in), or 2.1.2.1 giving 80 threads per 10 cm (approximately 19 ends per in). So one reed can give a number of dif-

ferent settings for the warp depending on how it is threaded.

If you decide to make your own table loom, the reed is probably the only specialist weaving part that you will have to buy. It is a better investment to buy stainless steel reeds, since they will not rust, though they are more expensive than ordinary ones. If you yourself do not want to make a loom, there are some reasonably priced looms in kit form on the market.

Just a quick note about the width of table looms. 40 cm (15 in) weaving width is about the narrowest that is of practical use — any looms narrower than this are probably designed for weaving samplers. The widest table loom that is practical is about 60 cm (24 in), because if they are any wider they tend to be rather awkward. The reason for this is that on a lot of table looms, the lifting mechanism is at the side of the loom, so that the weaver is constantly having to stretch out to reach the levers in order to lift each row. A wider loom also needs a large strong table on which to stand and cannot easily be moved around and stored when not in use. If you want to weave any wider than 60 cm (24 in), then it is best to invest in a foot loom.

PATTERN WEAVING

The main point about using a four-shaft loom is that you can weave some very interesting patterns. There are literally thousands of different patterns

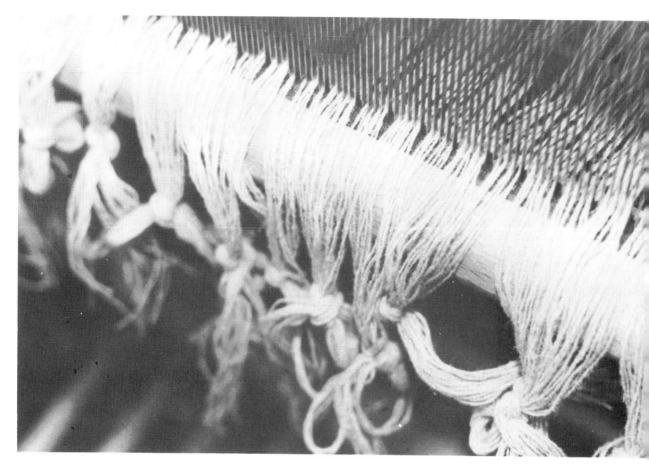

Photograph 33 Warp threads passing through
the reed and tied loosely in groups

and pattern variations, which all depend on the order in which the heddles are threaded and the shafts are lifted during weaving.

The simplest way of threading is 1, 2, 3, 4, and repeat this all the way across the warp. This means that the first thread is put through the first heddle on the shaft nearest the weaver. The second thread goes through the first heddle on the second shaft, etc. If shafts 1 and 3 are lifted together alternately with shafts 2 and 4, you get plain weave, since (with this threading sequence) each alternate thread is lifted. The advantage of

this system over the rigid heddle, is that on this same threading you can also weave many different patterns, just by altering the order and combination of lifting the shafts on each row. Twill weave is the most usual, this time lifting shafts 1 and 2, 2 and 3, 3 and 4, 4 and 1, repeat.

Both plain and twill weaves are shown in diagram form in figure 91. You will find similar diagrams in weaving pattern books, as this is the easiest way to show how to thread up and what the weave will be like. It is also useful as a way to make up your own patterns, using squared

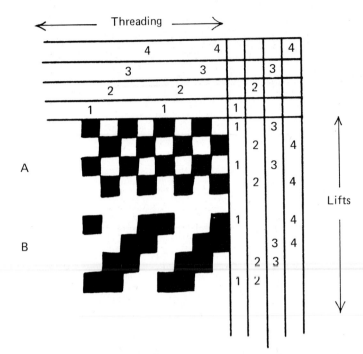

Figure 91 Four-shaft pattern drafts

threading sequence and shaft lifts. In practice, the only limitation is that in some weaves this will produce long loops of yarn not anchored into the fabric. These are known as overshots and large overshot designs were used in some of the American coverlets. If the design does have long overshots in it, think about the use to which it will be put before you weave. For example, if you have cats around the house they will probably love tearing the overshots on your upholstery material!

The other point to note is that some drafts are given for foot looms, where the shafts are pulled downwards. If you think that you are not getting the design you planned, try looking on the underneath of the weaving!

Generally speaking, the larger the pattern, the more carefully the finished article will have to be designed. If, for example there are only three pattern repeats over the whole width of the fabric, you must make sure that the designs are perfectly balanced, with the central panel exactly in the middle. Many of the traditional American designs were woven into coverlets.

There is not space in this book to list all the numerous patterns you can do on a four-shaft loom, and for further reference there are one or two pattern weaving books listed as recommended books. With more than four shafts, the possibilities are even greater. Usual combinations are eight-shaft, twelve-shaft or sixteen-shaft looms and it is possible to buy table looms with these numbers of shafts.

FOOT LOOMS

If you want to weave long lengths of cloth or anything wider than about 60 cm (24 in), then you really need a foot loom (also known as a floor loom or treadle loom). This is much quicker to weave on, as the shafts are tied up to pedals. As you press the pedals

paper. The way the shafts are threaded is shown along the top, and putting each shaft on a separate line makes the threading sequence easier to read at a glance. The way the shafts are lifted during weaving is shown in the right hand columns. To find out what the pattern will look like when woven, simply fill in the places where the warp will show in the finished piece; it is easiest if this is worked out on squared paper. For example, with plain weave, where in the right hand column there is a 1, look along the top and fill in the square underneath every 1 in the top row. For plain weave, shaft three is lifted at the same time, so all the 3s should also be filled in. That completes the first row, so then look at the second and fill in all the 2s and 4s. This produces the checkerboard design of plain weave.

In theory you can make up any threading you like by altering the

Photograph 34
Plain weave, showing
the effect of different
tones from white to
black in both warp
and weft

Photograph 35
Twill weave, showing
the way the pattern
stands out using a
white weft thread
on different tones of
warp from black to
white

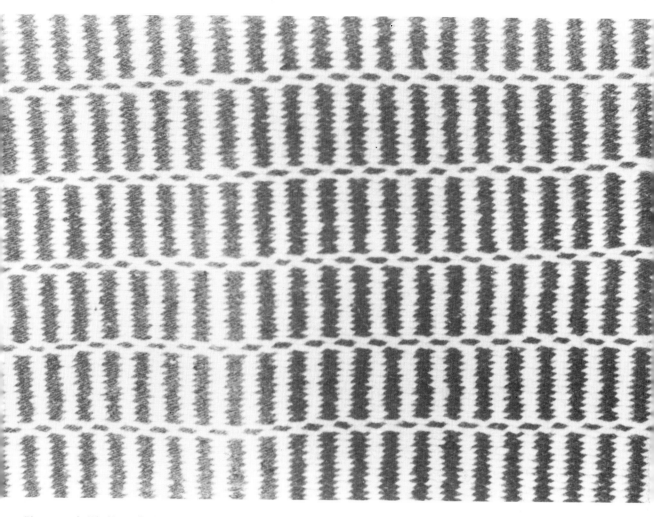

Photograph 36 Four-shaft rug weave

with your feet, the shafts are lifted, usually two at a time on a four-shaft loom. The pedals can be tied up to suit the weaver, so that if a series of lifts is repeated, the pedals are tied up in order to obtain this. A four-shaft foot loom usually has six pedals and the most usual tie-up is 1 and 3, 2 and 4 (for plain weave), 1 and 2, 2 and 3, 3 and 4 and 4 and 1 (for twill weave).

There are two types of foot loom, countermarch and counterbalance. On the counterbalance loom, the shafts are tied in pairs to rollers at the top. As one pedal is depressed, one shaft is pulled down and the other in the pair automatically rises. The counterbalance loom needs to be rather tall in order to have enough space at the top for the rollers to work properly and produce a good shed. The countermarch system is used on smaller looms, where there is not so much height needed to get a good shed. This works by jacks, which are pieces of wood which swivel at the top of the loom. The tie-up to the pedals is more complicated, because while one or more of the shafts are lifted, all the others are pulled down.

Another point to consider on a foot loom is whether the beater is overslung or underslung; the beater is the part of the loom which holds the reed in place. This is really a question of personal preference, but a heavy underslung beater is probably better for rugs. Incidentally, if you do want to weave rugs, make sure that you get a very strong loom, as the weft must be beaten into place very hard. Upright looms, specially designed for rug weaving with only two shafts for plain weave, are the best, and if you seriously want to specialize in making floor rugs, then it would be worthwhile making or buying one of these. Similar floor standing frames are available for tapestry, but these are not so strong and do not usually have pedals. If you want to concentrate on weaving hangings, then these upright frames take up much less space than a floor loom.

For a small house where space is a problem, it is possible to buy a fold-ing foot loom which is ideal for most home weavers, as it can be folded away when not in use. However, please note that most of these looms are not strong enough to weave rugs successfully, and the length of weaving is governed by the distance between the front roller and the front beam; the wider this gap, the more cloth can be wound on to the loom and this is particularly important if you intend to weave thick materials.

If you are seriously considering investing in a foot loom, then do shop around to see what is available. Check the prices to see exactly what accessories are included (heddles, reed, threading hooks, etc.) and bear in mind that you will also need a good warping mill, which will enable you to make much longer warps to put on the loom. If you decide to make the loom, then look at as many plans as possible, to make sure that you end up with a loom which will be suitable for your purpose.

Above all, whatever sort of weaving you decide to do, have fun! If you enjoy what you do, then the results will also give pleasure, both to yourself and to other people.

13 Selling Your Weaving

When you have really got hooked on weaving, and when you want to go on weaving but have made all the things you need around the house and have run out of friends to whom to give presents of weaving, the time has arrived to think about selling your work. Maybe friends have admired your work and have even commissioned you to weave them something similar. Of course you must have achieved some proficiency at the craft, but if people have really admired your weaving (and were not just trying to be tactful!), it is an indication that you might consider selling some of your products. But how and where do you start?

FINISHING YOUR WORK

The first step is to examine your own work as objectively as possible. Are the selvedges good? Are there any mistakes in the weaving? Are there knots or faults showing? If you can get a friend to give an honest critical opinion (without being afraid of ruining a beautiful friendship!), this can be very helpful. It is all too easy to overlook things which may not bother you if you were going to use the article. Just try to think: 'If I saw that in a shop, would I buy it? If so, why would I buy it? Why is it attractive? If not, why not?'

Of course you have to remember that you are not the eventual customer. Just because you like something, it does not mean that other people will like it as much. For example, you may make some lovely pink table mats, perfect in every detail, but it would be no good trying to sell them to me, because I have a prejudice against pink!

The overall appearance of the work is important, in order to attract the customer in the first place. This is not to say that every article you weave should be in bright colours. After all, a dull coloured scarf may stand out if displayed amongst brighter ones.

Detail is also important. The first step in trying to sell something is to get the customer's attention. Something about the article will stand out in the customer's mind and he or she will be drawn towards it. The next step is in the detail. If the customer is attracted by the colouring of a set of table mats which match exactly the colour scheme of the dining room, only to find on closer inspection that they are badly woven, then all the interest is lost.

Bad finishing can make a lovely handwoven article look like a disaster! To my mind, if you have taken all the time and trouble to weave something, equal care should be taken in finishing it off and making it up. On items such as table mats or towels, it is better to neatly handsew the seams. If your handsewing is uneven, machine stitches can be acceptable, but do take great care to match the thread as exactly as possible. I have seen numerous examples of badly machined handwork; it completely ruins the article and in many cases makes it look cheap and nasty.

If you intend to sell woollen tweed

lengths for the customer to make up, then do make sure that they are properly milled (shrunk) before they are sold. Small lengths can be done at home by pounding the tweed in soapflakes and water, until the fibres are matted together. Longer lengths can be put in the bath and trampled on until they are properly finished. The length should then be dried on a wooden roller, careful placing on this being essential to ensure that any stripes in the fabric are set straight. If you are contemplating weaving a lot of tweed, then it is probably better to send it away to have it milled professionally.

Of course, there may be some demand for handspun and natural dyed wool, both for embroidery and hand knitting. The wool must be thoroughly washed and if it is for knitting it should be plied. The wool should be neatly skeined or balled, and the natural colours often look very attractive displayed in a rush or cane basket.

Natural dyed wools can be a problem in that the dyes may not be very fast (permanent). Before selling, they should be thoroughly tested, first of all by washing a sample skein of wool several times and comparing any colour loss with a skein that has only been washed once. Exposure to light can also affect the dye, so try hanging a small skein up in a window in direct sunlight for at least several days to check. If you wrap half the skein in thick paper to prevent light from reaching part of it, you will be able to tell just how much it does fade. If there is any doubt about the fastness of the dye, a small label should be attached to each skein, explaining this to the customer.

Items such as handwoven scarves can have knotted fringes. Small groups of threads should be knotted together and the knots carefully placed in a straight line. It is just as well to wash any woollen item that may be greasy

or dirty. The knots should be tied before washing (to prevent the weft unravelling), but the fringes cut evenly at both ends after it has been washed and ironed. Wool should be washed by hand and in pure soapflakes.

When you are selling your work, you should be aware of the Trades Descriptions Act. According to this act, an article must be fit for the purpose for which it is described. So a rug, for example, should be hardwearing and not made of such soft yarns that it disintegrates quickly. It is always just as well to attach a label to your work listing the fibre content of the article and giving brief washing instructions. This is particularly important, as most handwoven articles must be carefully washed by hand. A customer who inadvertently bundles your precious handweaving into the washing machine may be rather disappointed at the results!

The presentation of the work is very important. A neatly printed label giving your name and address (essential advertising if you want to attract further business) is better than a badly written one. If you can afford to have some sew-in labels printed, this is a permanent reminder for the satisfied customer.

WHAT TO WEAVE

This will depend on the type of things you can make well and the kind of market for which you are aiming. There is no doubt that small items sell more quickly than large ones. For example, you will probably be able to sell many more bookmarks than bedspreads; the bookmark can be an impulse buy, whereas the bedspread often needs careful consideration before a purchase is made. On the other hand, you will need to sell a lot of bookmarks in order to make as much profit as you would by selling one bedspread.

What you decide to weave is in

Photograph 37 Child's skirt, woven in knitting wool by Evelyn Green

many ways tied up with the kind of market you find, and more details on finding this are given in the next section. The main thing is to find something that you enjoy producing and which will sell. Unless you become one of the country's top professional weavers, you are unlikely to make your fortune out of weaving, so that enjoyment plays a major factor.

The type of loom you have will also dictate what kind of work you can do. If you have an inkle loom, then belts, ties and bookmarks are the obvious lines to try and perfect. Remember that once you become proficient at doing something it gets progressively easier and quicker to achieve a professional finish. Bookmarks are a good line because they can be sold fairly cheaply, and several can be set up on an inkle loom at the same time, thus needing only one lot of threading up.

On the whole it is better to make finished articles, rather than just trying to sell lengths of woven material. The everyday items such as scarves, bags, ties, belts, bookmarks and table mats usually sell well, provided that they are different from the machine-made items that can be bought. In handweaving, the weaver can be compared to an artist in yarn and should aim to create a unique style.

Wall hangings are a more risky venture, but the rewards can be quite high. If you decide to concentrate on wall hangings, then you are really painting a picture in yarn. Your wall hanging should be unique and can therefore sell for a high price if it is well done. But remember that they are usually more difficult to sell, as they have to appeal to just the right buyer.

There is a great challenge in weaving a particular item for a particular place, taking great care in matching colours, and creating a design that will fit in with its future surroundings.

This type of weaving, whether for furnishing fabrics, rugs, cushions, etc., can be very rewarding and can command a high price, but there are pitfalls to commission weaving.

Firstly you have to find your customers either by advertising or by word of mouth (satisfied customers telling their friends). Either way, you have to get known and there are no short cuts to this. Take every opportunity to show your work at exhibitions and craft fairs. Doing demonstrations and giving lectures about weaving and spinning can also help. You will also have to build up a good portfolio of samples and photographs of your work, to show prospective customers.

When you start commissions, it can be hard work. A good deal of time needs to be spent in preliminary planning, and consultations with the customer can take many hours, until you reach a decision on the final form the design will take. You may have to quote a finished price, and this can take more time to work out the cost of materials, etc. And when you have done all this work, including possibly weaving some samples, be prepared for the customer who changes his or her mind or even cancels the order. However, if you can persevere, the rewards in both money and job satisfaction can make it all worthwhile!

Colour can play a very important part in selling your work. Have you thought about what colours are in fashion at the moment? When you have sold a few things, you will start to see that certain colours sell better than others and other colours will not sell at all. Bear this in mind when doing your next lot of weaving.

Though it is good to have a high aim in view, start by making those things that you do best, and then expand so that you have a good range of items to sell. It is only by trying new ideas that you will find out what sells. Scarves, ties, bags and bookmarks may sound very ordinary, but if you can experiment and create your own unique style, then you are on the right lines.

HOW TO FIND THE RIGHT MARKET

Start by looking around your local shops. Is there a craft shop? If it does not have any handweaving, maybe the owner would like to try some? If there is some already, then is your work different enough to be able to contrast with what is already there? It is better to start locally, not only because it is easier to keep an eye on your own work, but also because if the shop is dealing with the tourist market, there is an added attraction for them to be able to sell something made locally.

If the right kind of shop is not available locally, then go further afield. It is always a good idea to visit as many craft shops as possible. Look carefully and critically at what they sell, how the goods are displayed and the sort of prices being asked. If you think that there might be a place for your goods in a particular shop, then it is a good idea to approach the owner. Have a good look around the shop first and if possible find out the name of the owner or buyer. Do not approach the buyer straight away — he or she is probably so used to seeing sales representatives that saying 'No' becomes a habit!

Always make a proper appointment to see the buyer; after all he/she cannot give you full attention if the shop is full of customers who need to be dealt with at the same time, and the customers have to come first! Probably a preliminary telephone call is best, arranging a time when it is convenient for the buyer to see you and give you undivided attention. Explain that you have visited the shop, were impressed with the items on sale (a little flattery never did any harm and if you did not like the shop you would not want your handweaving to be associated with it anyway!), and would like to show him/her some of your work.

On the day, arrive in good time, and with a good selection of items to show. Do not be put off if the buyer is not as enthusiastic about your work as you would wish. Ask his opinion of it and whether or not he or she could find a place for it in the shop. Be prepared for disappointments before you find success, and always listen and take note of what buyers tell you. They know what they can and cannot sell, and if you show that you are willing to adapt, you may find a more favourable outcome.

The pricing of handweaving will be dealt with more fully in the next section, but it would be useful to put in a word or two here about leaving items on 'sale or return'. Chances are that if you are approaching a craft shop for the first time, you may be invited to leave your work on sale or return. This means that you will be paid only when the work is sold to a retail customer, but it will be returned to you after an agreed period if it does not sell. This leaves you with the risk of having work lying in the shop, but no money coming in immediately. On the other hand, it is better to have your work on show to the public, than locked away in a chest at home. Buyers will be more willing to take your work if you let them have it on sale or return, because they will not have to risk their own money on items that they are not sure of selling. And if later on you find a better outlet, you can just as quickly get your handweaving back, in order to put it somewhere more profitable.

Finding exactly the right market is not easy. What you consider to be the right setting may not be where other people see your work. Try to be as objective as possible and look at your weaving as if you were a com-

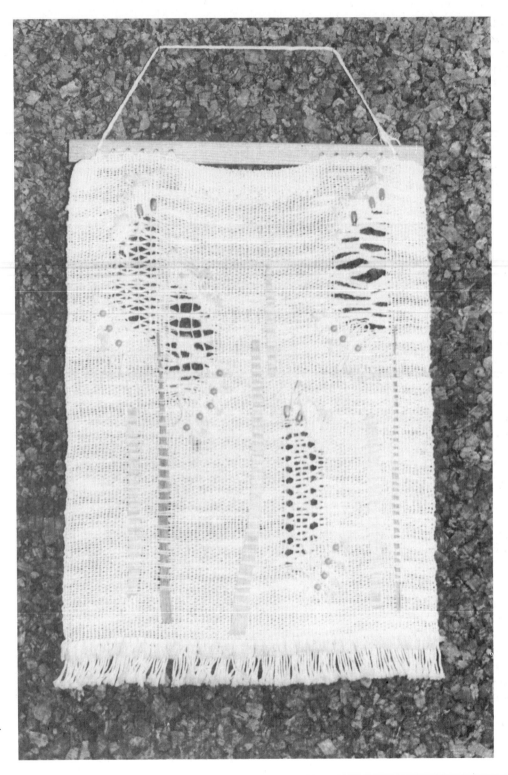

Photograph 38
Woven and embroid-
ered hanging, by
Evelyn Green

plete stranger seeing it for the first time. Ask someone else's opinion. Does it look as though it was bought in a gallery or a jumble sale? The answer probably lies somewhere between these two extremes.

Another way to sell your work, if you have enough or can club together with a few other crafts people, is to organize an exhibition. The other crafts need not be weaving; in fact, different crafts often complement each other, such as weaving, pottery and woodwork. The venue for this is very important; it must be easily accessible to the public and well publicized in advance. If you hire a hall, make sure the terms allow you actually to sell your work. This way of selling your work can be very rewarding, as you come face to face with your customers (but be prepared for some unwelcome comments as well!). The snag is that you will have to lay out money in advance on renting the hall, getting posters and handouts printed (or maybe one of the craftsmen is a printer?) and insuring all the exhibits (very important, against accidental damage and pilfering). It also takes a great deal of time and effort in getting the whole thing organized, arranging the exhibits and manning the exhibition while it is open to the public. It is a gamble — but like all gambles, it might just pay off!

Joining your local crafts group may be useful, so that you can participate in their exhibitions. You will not have nearly so much work as in organizing your own exhibition, but you will probably be able to put only a limited number of pieces on show. There may also be selection procedures, so be prepared for disappointment. Again, make sure before you agree to exhibit that you will be allowed to sell your work, and find out what commission is deducted from sale prices.

Sometimes there are craft fairs held and you may be able to rent a stall just for a day or two at a reasonable price. This is also worth considering, but bear in mind the kind of people who attend and the kind of things they are likely to buy.

If this section strikes rather a pessimistic note and makes you aware of some of the pitfalls involved, then it has achieved its purpose. Remember that unless you are very lucky, there is a long hard road to success and even some of the best known artists have had to struggle to achieve recognition. Nevertheless it can be very enjoyable and rewarding selling your own work, provided you are willing to take help and advice as you go along. Even if you can just make your hobby self-financing, it is a very good start.

WHAT TO CHARGE

Anyone reading this section in the hope of finding a magic formula on pricing will be disappointed! Pricing handmade goods is very difficult and having been involved in the retailing of crafts for some years, I still do not know the answer! Even if one could work out a rigid system of what applies to one shop, it would not necessarily apply in a different shop in a different location.

Bear in mind that if you charge a reasonable amount for your labour time, you will probably price your weaving too high to sell easily. Even if your hobby can only be self-financing, it still helps and any profit on top of that is a bonus. That at least is the pessimistic point of view!

In order to work out a reasonable price, start with the yarn used. Calculate how much it would cost you today to buy the same yarn to repeat the same article. There are two reasons for doing this. One is that even if the yarn was bought in a sale for next-to-nothing, you must take into account its 'real' cost now, in order to get enough money back to buy more yarn. With inflation, the price charged for an article woven with yarn bought some time ago must reflect its replacement value today. To take an extreme example, let us say you have woven a scarf and sold it very cheaply because the yarn was given to you by a friend. A friend of the customer who bought it wants one exactly the same and you find that in order to do this you will have to buy more yarn at its true market cost. Do you accept the commission for the scarf, but try and explain to the customer that it will cost twice the price her friend paid, or do you weave the scarf at a loss and write it down to experience? This sort of situation is not likely to happen very often, but it illustrates the point.

After you have worked out the cost of the yarn, you should add a reasonable amount on for all the time and skill involved in making it. But how do you define 'reasonable'? This is where there is no definite answer, as the market will tend to dictate the price. If you have a high class outlet, then you can ask a high price, but the local village craft shop may not attract the kind of customers who can afford high prices. Here is where you need to do some homework. Visit as many different craft shops as you can and compare quality and prices with the location of the shop. Hang around for a while if you can and see the type of people who come into the shop and buy! Listening to their comments can be very helpful.

Once you have established a reasonable price for your woven goods, remember that the shopkeeper also has his overheads and needs to make a profit in order just to keep in business. If you halve the price of the goods on the shelf, you will be somewhere near the mark of what you can expect to receive. The shop's mark-up (the difference between what you are selling the article for and the price the retail customer will have to pay) will vary from place to place. The larger the shop and the nearer the centre of town, the higher profit the shopkeeper needs just to cover expenses. After all, he or she is providing you with a place to exhibit your work and staff who will help to sell it, so you have to pay for this service somehow. Always ask the shop owner what percentage mark-up is added, and make sure that he or she does not work it the other way around, using your price as the selling price, so you end up with less than you thought!

If you have your own stall or exhibition, you need to charge higher prices, as you will have to foot the bill for all the expenses, whether or not you sell anything. But once again, what you decide to charge depends on your location. You will get less from a village fête than from a nationally sponsored craft fair. The only way to find out is to try. If you did not sell much weaving on one occasion, was it because the prices were too high? If you sold most of the work, then that is good, but maybe the prices were too cheap and did not really cover all the hidden expenses.

At the beginning it is wisest to keep your prices as low as you can without being out of pocket. After all, it is better to sell some work and be able to afford to buy more yarn with the proceeds, than to have a huge pile of weaving mounting up and no money coming in. It also gives your confidence a tremendous boost to sell something. Begin slowly and as you see how things sell, adjust your prices so that you just keep a steady turnover at a reasonable profit, without pricing yourself out of the market.

One thing you should beware of, and that is the attitude of some people who think that because an article is handmade it should be cheap. If it is unique and well made, it can command a high price. Do not put

Photograph 39
Hanging (woven sideways) incorporating wooden drops, woven by Evelyn Green

your prices up and down just because other people tell you to, but rely on the information you get from selling your own work or how a shop sells it on your behalf. If you are selling all the table mats you can make, then it makes nonsense to reduce the price, but if you are not selling them, then you must either change their outlet or think about whether the price is contributing to their lack of sales.

Above all, it is worth taking considerable time and trouble to get the right price and the right outlet for your handweaving. Unless you are very lucky it will take time and a lot of experimenting, until you hit on the right spot. However, be patient and do not give up even after several disappointments. Good luck!

19 How to Continue

It is hoped that by the time you reach this chapter, you have not only read and enjoyed looking through this book, but have tried at least one or two of the types of weaving described. If this book has achieved its aim in getting you interested in weaving, then you will by now be asking: 'What next?'

First of all, consult the list of recommended books at the end. Brief notes are given on most of the books where the titles are not self-explanatory, and if there is a technique that you particularly enjoyed, then it would be a good idea to follow this up first. Most of these books were in print at the time this book was written, but where there was no comprehensive book on a particular subject available (for example on inkle weaving), there are books listed which you can probably obtain from your local library. This list of books only scratches the surface of available literature, and there are many other weaving books available. The ones included in the list are ones I can recommend for one reason or another, but any weaving books you can get hold of will help.

There are also several specialist magazines on the market, mainly available by postal subscription. These usually contain a wide range of topics related to the three crafts (weaving, spinning and dyeing), articles for beginners and general interest items, advertisements and news of classes and courses. Addresses of the publishers are also given.

Having got hooked on weaving, you may like to meet other weavers. In England, the Association of Guilds of Weavers, Spinners and Dyers has branches in most of the counties. They welcome anyone interested in weaving, from beginners to professional weavers, and provide a point of contact for weavers to get together. Often there are regular meetings (probably once a month) where guest speakers may give helpful lectures, classes may be organized, outings to places of interest and exhibitions of members' work. The address of the head office of the association is given on page 117, and they will be able to give you the name and address of the secretary of your nearest guild.

It is always helpful to see other people demonstrating crafts. Keep a look out in your local newspaper for details of any craft fairs, particularly ones where there are demonstrations. Sometimes if you cannot fully understand a technique from a book, it can all come clear when you see someone actually doing it.

Also, if you can attend a class, this is very helpful. Approach your local art college and see if they can offer you anything. There may be private classes run locally, and the secretary of your local guild should be able to let you have any information about this. Another idea is to combine a holiday with learning to weave. There are many such residential schools advertized in the national craft magazines, and there is a lot to be said in favour of having a few uninterrupted days to concentrate on something you enjoy. Most courses should be able to offer a brochure or leaflet giving details of their programme, but the best way not to be disappointed is to go by personal recommendation. If you can attend one or two guild meetings and ask around, you may be able to find out whether or not the courses are as good as they say they are on the advertising brochure!

Suppliers of weaving and spinning equipment should help you if they can; it is after all in their own interests to encourage you to weave, so that you will buy your supplies from them in future! A short list of suppliers is given at the end of this book. They may have equipment on show and even woven examples. They may run classes or at least be able to tell you how to find out where there may be some. Most important of all, if you are considering buying a loom, they should be able to help you decide what you need for your requirements. For example, if you want to weave rugs, you will need a very sturdy loom, as rugs have to be beaten very hard in order to produce a firm hard-wearing surface.

Perhaps the best way to continue is to talk about weaving. You may find you have friends who become interested and would like to club together to make or buy a loom. Who knows, you may find that someone you know does weaving as a hobby, and you never realized! Weaving can be a solitary occupation, but if you can communicate through your work and find like-minded people with whom to discuss your hobby, it can be a very enjoyable pastime and one with endless possibilities.

Glossary

Card Weaving — using small shaped pieces of cardboard as the loom, not to be confused with tablet weaving, where the warp is threaded through small cards.

Carders — pair of wooden 'bats' covered on one side with wire hooks, used for making fibres parallel prior to spinning.

Cross Sticks — pair of sticks with a hole at each end, used for holding the warp cross in position while threading.

E.P.CM. — ends (warp threads) per centimetre.

E.P.I. — ends (warp threads) per inch.

Fish Hook — reed hook.

Fleece — wool fibres shorn from the sheep.

Heddles — loops of string or metal, used to lift selected warp threads.

Loom — any piece of equipment that will support a set of parallel threads at an even tension for weaving.

Mordant — a chemical used in dyeing, which helps the yarn to absorb more of the dyestuff.

Pick-up Technique — any technique where extra warp threads are manipulated by hand or with a stick to form a pattern.

Plain Weave — darning, where alternate threads pass over and under each other.

Ply — the number of threads twisted together to form a yarn; 3-ply yarn thus consists of three threads plied together. (N.B. Knitting yarn plies correspond to a certain thickness and do not necessarily contain the stated number of threads, so a 4-ply knitting yarn may not always have four strands.)

Raddle — device for spacing the warp threads quickly, used when winding the warp on to the loom.

Reed — device for spacing the warp threads evenly on the loom and for beating the weft threads into place.

Rolag — long round 'sausage' of parallel fibres, ready for spinning.

Shafts — metal or wooden frames, which hold the heddles in position.

Shed — gap between two sets of warp threads when heddles are raised or lowered, through which the shuttle passes.

Shed Stick — flat wooden stick, used at the beginning of weaving.

Shuttle — wooden stick, around which the weft thread is wound.

Spindle — a stick and a weight, used for spinning.

Substantive Dye — dye that can be used without a mordant.

Tapestry — woven tapestry, weft-faced fabric, not to be confused with canvas work (needlework tapestry).

Teasing — separating the fibres prior to spinning.

Thrums — short ends of warp yarn left over when the cloth is cut off the loom, usually refers to carpet yarn.

Warp — the threads of yarn wound on the loom prior to weaving.

Warp-faced Fabric — one where only the warp threads are visible (inkle weaving, finger weaving).

Weft — yarn passed over and under the warp threads to hold them together. (One way to remember this is to think of the WEFT thread passing from WEST to EAST!)

Weft-faced Fabric — one where only the weft threads are visible (tapestry weaving).

Whorl — the weight on the spindle, usually a round disc of wood.

Bibliography

Beutlich, Tadek, *The Technique of Woven Tapestry*, Batsford, 2nd edition, 1969

British Wool Marketing Board, *British Sheep Breeds*, Bradford, 1978
Good photographs and descriptions of the main British sheep breeds

Brooke, Jess, *Tapestry Weaving*, Robert Hale, 1975
Good, clear introduction

Brown, Rachel, *The Weaving, Spinning and Dyeing Book*, Routledge and Kegan Paul, 1979
Good introduction to all types of weaving

Burt, Jocelyn, *Patterns for Weaving*, Robert Hale, 1975
Mostly four-shaft patterns

Chadwick, Eileen, *The Craft of Handspinning*, Batsford, 1980
Good text and well illustrated

Davenport, Elsie G., *Your Handspinning*, Select Books, Ojai, California, 1964 edition
Good text

Davison, Marguerite Porter, *A Handweaver's Pattern Book*, M. Davison, Publisher, Swarthmore, Pa., 19th edition, 1977
Excellent book with illustrations and instructions to weave hundreds of four-shaft patterns

Field, Anne, *Weaving with the Rigid Heddle Loom*, Batsford, 1980

Gordon, Linda, *Weaving on Card and Board Looms*, Dryad Press, Leicester, 1976
Coloured leaflet

Gourlat, Catherine, *Weaving in Style*, Mills and Boon, 1980
Instructions for weaving clothes, mostly using plain weave

Green, David and Ashburner, Jenni, *Dyes from the Kitchen*, Batsford, 1979
How to use materials found around the home to obtain natural dyes

Hart, Edward, *Sheepkeeping on a Small Scale*, Thorsons Publishers, Wellingborough, 1979

Hjert, Jeri and Von Rosenstiel, Paul, *Loom Construction*, Van Nostrand Reinhold, 1978
Working drawings and instructions for making a variety of looms

Holland, Nina, *Inkle Loom Weaving*, Pitman, 1973 — out of print

Jacobs, Betty E.M., *Growing Herbs and Plants for Dyeing*, Select Books, Ojai, California, 1977

Kahn, Deborah (Ed), *The Handspun Project Book*, Select Books, Ojai, California, 1978
Ideas on how to use your handspun wool for weaving, knitting and crochet

Kilbride, Thomas, *Spinning and Weaving at Home*, Thorsons Publishers, Wellingborough, 1980
Making and using home-made equipment

Miles, Vera, *Weaving Patterns for the Two-way Loom*, Dryad Press, Leicester, 4th edition, 1974
How to make patterns in plain weave by using colour changes

Miles, Vera, *Practical Four-shaft Weaving*, Dryad Press, Leicester, 3rd edition, 1979
Instructions for making 14 useful articles

Murray, Rosemary, *Practical Modern*

Weaving, Van Nostrand Reinhold, 1975
Good, clear instructions for rigid heddle and four-shaft looms

Paulin, Lynn, *Weaving for Beginners*, Gick Publishing Inc., Laguna Hills, California, 1977
Clear instructions for using frame looms

Paulin, Lynn, *Weaving on Rings and Hoops*, Gick Publishing Inc., Laguna Hills, California, 1978

Redman, Jane, *Frame Loom Weaving*, Van Nostrand Reinhold, 1976

Robertson, Seonaid, *Dyes from Plants*, Van Nostrand Reinhold, 1973

Smith, Frances B., *Inkle Loom Weaving*, Sterling Publishing Co., New York, 1976 — out of print

Taber, Barbara and Anderson, Lynn, *Backstrap Weaving*, Pitman, 1975

Thurstan, Violetta, *The Use of Vegetable Dyes*, Dryad Press, Leicester, 15th edition, 1977

Turner, Alta R., *Finger Weaving: Indian Braiding*, Sterling Publishing Co., New York, 1973

Wickens, Hetty M., *Wool Spinning*, Dryad Press, Leicester, 1978
Coloured leaflet

Wickens, Hetty M., *Vegetable or Natural Dyeing in Wool*, Dryad Press, Leicester, 1978
Coloured leaflet

Wickens, Hetty M., *Weaving: Designing with the Rigid Heddle*, Dryad Press, Leicester, 1978
Coloured leaflet on ideas to use the rigid heddle

Wilson, Jean, *Weaving is for Anyone*, Van Nostrand Reinhold, 1967

Wilson, Jean, *Weaving You Can Use*, Van Nostrand Reinhold, 1975

WEAVING MAGAZINES

Loomcraft, quarterly, articles of general interest to weavers, plus instructions on how to weave articles.
Campden Weavers, 16 Lower High Street, Chipping Campden, Gloucestershire GL55 6DY

Weavers Journal, quarterly, articles of general interest to weavers, plus occasional articles on basic techniques and guild reports.
The Secretary, *Weavers Journal*, Association of Guilds of Weavers, Spinners and Dyers, BCM 963, London WC1N 3XX.

Spindle, Shuttle and Dyepot, quarterly Handweavers Guild of America, P.O. Box 7–374, 65 La Salle Road, West Hartford, Conn, 06107, U.S.A.

Suppliers

NORTHERN CALIFORNIA HAND-
WEAVERS SUPPLY, 111 East Spain
Street, On the Alley, Sonoma, Ca.
95476
    Weaving and spinning supplies
NORWOOD LOOMS, P.O. Box 167,
Fremont, MI 49412
    Looms
SCHACHT SPINDLE CO. INC., P.O.
Box 2157K, Boulder, Co. 80306
    Looms

SCOTT'S WOOLEN MILL, Elmdale
Road, Uxbridge, Mass. 01569
    Yarns
WOVENWARE, 1810 North Orange
Avenue, Orlando, Florida 32804
    Weaving supplies
YARN 'N SHUTTLE, 199 So. High-
land, Memphis, Tenn, 38111
    Weaving supplies

Index